Hilarious tale of an international banker who, through trials and tribulations, fell in love with Africa at the turn of the millennium.
Robert Masumboko | Country Director, Benin, African Development Bank (AfDB)

It Began in Africa is a captivating, humorous, and eye-opening memoir that offers rare insight into life, politics, and business across post-colonial Africa from the vantage point of a young Pakistani banker. Rizwan Haider brings the continent to life with vivid anecdotes, humility, and reverence for the people and cultures he encountered. His stories—ranging from Cold War intrigues to linguistic misadventures and cultural revelations—shine with humanity and wit. This book is not a scholarly treatise, but it is rich with lived truth and personal growth. It reminds us that understanding, respect, and curiosity are essential for meaningful cross-cultural engagement.
Carl Grant III | Author, How to Live the Abundant Life

Through well-articulated anecdotes and thought-provoking observations, Haider's memoir provides a refreshing perspective on the State of Africa over the last four decades.
European diplomat on assignment in West Africa

An engaging memoir that provides a nuanced understanding of the challenges and opportunities in Africa's public sector.
Tamara Nall | CEO & Founder, The Leading Niche

Rizwan's memoir offers an educational glimpse into Africa's diverse cultures and histories—perfect for enriching any curriculum on global studies.
Kumar R. Parakala | USA National best-selling author, Lead to Disrupt

Rizwan Haider smoothly balances social and economical analysis with personal anecdotes, making this memoir an exciting introspection into a world usually confined to private bankers' diners. From voodoo spells to flying with retired mercenaries or the quagmire that is the Franc CFA reform, the reader is smoothly taken into a journey throughout the other side of Africa's financial life. It is a delightful read for both insiders and outsiders.

Yena Apithy | Vice President, Trader (Japan and Asian Markets), Morgan Stanley MUFG

IT BEGAN IN AFRICA

A Banker's Memoirs From The Heartland!

RIZWAN HAIDER

Copyright © 2025 Rizwan Haider

Published in the United States by Leaders Press.

www.leaderspress.com

All rights reserved. No part of this book may be reproduced or transmitted in any form or by any means, electronic or mechanical, including photocopying, recording, or by an information storage and retrieval system – except by a reviewer who may quote brief passages in a review to be printed in a magazine or newspaper – without permission in writing from the publisher.

All trademarks, service marks, trade names, product names, and logos appearing in this publication are the property of their respective owners.

ISBN 978-1-63735-343-1 (hcv)

ISBN 978-1-63735-342-4 (pbk)

ISBN 978-1-63735-341-7 (ebook)

Library of Congress Control Number: **2024916506**

Table of Contents

Introduction 9

CHAPTER 1: ARRIVAL IN AFRICA 15
    It Was a Dark and Stormy Night – 1979 15
    Gabon Circa 1979 20

CHAPTER 2: THE WORDS GET IN THE WAY 25
    (Mis)Communication in Africa – 1980 25

CHAPTER 3: COLD WAR AND AFRICA 37
    Financing of Proxy Battles on the Continent – 1980 37

CHAPTER 4: RELICS OF THE COLONIAL ERA 49
    4.1 A Visit to Dr. Schweitzer's Hospital, Lambarene, Gabon – 1981 49
    4.2 A Memorable Cricket Match 58

CHAPTER 5: THE WINNER TAKES IT ALL 65
    A Gambler's Tale – 1981 65

CHAPTER 6: A FLYING ADVENTURE 73
    Elephants and Planes – 1982 73

CHAPTER 7: AN APARTHEID STORY 79
    How to Become an Honorary White Person – 1986 79

CHAPTER 8: THE HIDDEN SIDE OF AFRICA: SECRET SOCIETIES, VOODOO, MAGIC . 89
    Watching Voodoo Spells Unfold Firsthand – 1993 89

CHAPTER 9: WHEN THINGS GO WRONG 95
    A Comedy of Confusions – 1994 95

CHAPTER 10: AN UNFORGETTABLE GIFT 101
    Crocodile Handy – 1994 101

CHAPTER 11: SCAMS IN AFRICA 109
    The Nigerian Mail Fraud Story – 1995 109
    "I am you, you are not me": A Story of Stolen
    Identity – 1998 115

**CHAPTER 12: A CLOSE ENCOUNTER WITH
DISASTER** 123
    Crash Landing in Rubber Plantations – 1998 123

CHAPTER 13: IT HAPPENS A LOT IN AFRICA 129
    How to Survive a Military Coup – 1999 129

CHAPTER 14: I NEED A MAP 137
    Are We in Africa? 137

CHAPTER 15: CANADA DISCOVERS ANGOLA 143
    First Canadian Delegation – 2006 143
    My Boss Visits Angola with Me 149

CHAPTER 16: HE CAME, HE SAW, HE CONQUERED! ... 155
    Story of a Legendary Mercenary – 2006 155

**CHAPTER 17: FRENCH-SPEAKING AFRICA –
THE CFA MONETARY ZONE** 165
    Myths and Mistakes 165

CHAPTER 18: JOYS OF TRAVELING IN AFRICA 181
    Landing in Lagos When the City Was Shut
    Down – 2007 181
    A Visit to Congo-Kinshasa (ex-Zaire) 187
    A Visit to Equatorial Guinea 191

CHAPTER 19: YOUR BUSINESS IS MINE! 199
    Everyone Wants Africa's Natural Resources 199

CHAPTER 20: THE LAST WORD 207

About the Author 211

IT BEGAN IN AFRICA!

Introduction

Life happens. And if it has been happening for several decades, one is bound to have accumulated a lot of stories. People have often told me that I should write mine down, yet I have taken that advice with a grain of salt. Those people are part of a small group of friends and well-wishers. They would give me words of encouragement after a nice dinner when everyone was in very good spirits. I had told myself that their opinions about my stories were obviously biased, so I should not take them seriously. Ironically, the encouragement of friends initially kept me from pursuing the project.

The other obstacle, quite surprising to me, was the actual writing part. I had thought that if I wanted to write my stories, well, all I would need is the time. On vacation, on a couple of occasions, the spirit did take me, and I tried to write, only to be distracted by the TV or the Internet. But I told myself that a time would come when the stories would write themselves if I wanted them to.

Still, the question may be asked: apart from the gentle nudges from friends, what was the true motive behind this book, and why should anyone read it? The serious answer to this question is that I have some very interesting stories about the African continent to tell, based on my several decades of observation and experience as an expatriate banker. My stories carry a personal firsthand view of the events. Some of them are very personal. Others narrate historical events from my perspective. You may read and enjoy these stories and move on to other matters. Or develop a deeper interest in Africa's affairs. It is entirely up to you.

It was in 2023 that I realized that I had to take the bull by the horns. After all, how hard could it be? I have been writing throughout my entire life. To motivate myself, I made a list of everything that I have written over the last forty years. This list included loan proposals, investment memorandums, credit analyses, performance reviews, risk management policies, compliance manuals, feasibility studies, structured finance deal papers, term sheets, risk management procedures, audit reports, macroeconomic reviews, etc. My reports have always been commended by my bosses, members of the boards of directors, and corporate clients. I thought I would read some of them to find inspiration. But the words that jumped at me in those documents looked like this: "amortization, asset allocation, debt to equity ratio, collateral, compound interest, joint and several liabilities, risk asset acceptance criteria, etc." And phrases such as, "The slowdown is expected to accelerate in the third quarter." These were my words, my phrases, and my world when it came to writing.

Unfortunately, to write my stories, they were of no use at all. I wanted to write them "in the simplest fashion with a touch of humor"—these were the exact words that I told my consultant when I seriously embarked upon this book project. So, this is what I have tried to do. Just sit at my desk and type the stories on my laptop. This book is a series of stories from my life in Africa.

But let me caution you: I have not attempted to write an autobiography. My life is not interesting enough to present in thorough detail to you, dear reader. However, very much like everybody else, I have been a witness to happenings that are worth telling.

I grew up in Karachi, Pakistan. When I obtained my bachelor of commerce degree, I had a very conventional path for my professional career, in my mind. I wanted to become a chartered accountant. This required an internship with an accounting firm and a five-year work and study program. I had started my internship in a traditional firm called Ford, Rhodes, Robson, Morrow. It was during that time that a senior cousin of mine showed me an ad from an international bank. They were looking for young graduates with careers in international banking. I had very little idea what it entailed, but it sounded way more exciting than Ford, Rhodes... you get the picture. I was selected by the bank, and that is how my adventure began.

I arrived in Africa forty-five years ago, in early 1979. It was a different world back then. The Iron Curtain divided the world into two camps. There were no mobile phones and no internet. I arrived in the former French colony of Gabon and lived there for six years, working as an expatriate in an international bank. This was the period when I established my understanding and appreciation for Africa, and it has lasted a lifetime.

After Gabon, I lived in several other African countries and traveled to many others over the years. I have observed and studied the history, politics, and many cultures and people in Africa. I have seen the impact of the past interactions between the so-called civilized world and the continent in the form of slave trade, colonization, and neo-colonialism. However, my observations do not qualify me to write an

Most African countries gained independence in the 1960s. The current borders of the African states were mostly decided during the late nineteenth century by the colonial powers back then. The division of the continent seems arbitrary and sometimes very weird. As an example of weird, here is the location of the country called The Gambia ("The" is an integral part of the name of the country. If you don't add it when referring to the country, the Gambians get very upset):

As you may have noticed, The Gambia is a country inserted inside Senegal with an opening in the Atlantic Ocean. The Gambia is a former British colony, whereas Senegal is a former French colony. Apparently, the British imposed upon the French to provide them access to the French territory through The Gambia River, including some land on both sides of that river, for the purposes of trading. This country gained independence with the same colonial borders. My first trip to The Gam-

It Began In Africa

> bia in the 1980s was so uneventful that I did not notice I was passing through it. I was visiting the southernmost region of Senegal called Casamance by road. We stopped at one point, and we had to board a ferry with the car to go to the other side. That was it. I had crossed the country and the river, both named Gambia. I noticed the river very well but did not perceive that I had also crossed the country.

academic book. This book is not a scholarly account of the history, geography, economics, or socio-cultural dynamics of Africa. In fact, it is not a scholarly account of anything at all. In the interest of full disclosure, I must confess that this book is not going to make you an expert in African affairs. It will not provide you with any tools to apply for a job as a diplomat or a foreign affairs expert. You will find nothing of that sort here, far from it even. I simply want to give a very personal glimpse of some aspects of the massive, extremely complex, and diverse continent of Africa. I have a profound respect for the continent and its people. My commentary is not in any manner intended to mock the people or the continent.

While telling my stories, I have tried to provide some context where needed so that you, who may not be very familiar with the history and politics of Africa, could appreciate these tales. I'll try very hard not to be longwinded and boring.

When I was first told by my employer that I was going to work in Africa, I was a twenty-year-old Pakistani lad with a finance degree. My knowledge and understanding of the continent were extremely limited. I had a cousin who had lived in Tanzania and Nigeria on World Bank assignments, and I had seen an American TV series called *Daktari* (1966-69) set in Kenya. The show was about an American physician and his family who provided medical assistance to wild animals. Also, there was an international conference of the Muslim heads of state in 1974 in Lahore, Pakistan, where most African countries with a significant Muslim population were represented by their heads of state. I followed that event on TV as a student and watched personalities such as Omar Kaddafi of Libya, Idi Amin of Uganda, Houari

Boumedienne of Algeria, and Anwar Sadat of Egypt. But none of this gave me any clear idea of what life in Africa would be like.

I was told that my likely location for the assignment would be in Francophone Africa. The term "Francophone" in itself sounded intimidating, but I soon found out that it was a fancy term for "French-speaking." I had no idea about the linguistic landscape of the continent at the time, and it dawned on me how little I knew. Being a nerd of the '70s, I went to the British Council library. I asked the librarian to suggest some books about Africa. He looked at me with his reading glasses, sitting almost at the tip of his nose. He suggested a few books, one of which was *The Heart of Darkness* by Joseph Conrad. I needed some practical information quickly, hence I was not going to plunge into the world of literary fiction to learn the basic facts about Africa. The Encyclopedia Britannica was my best bet. I would read *The Heart of Darkness* a couple of years later while I was already living in Africa.

When I told the librarian that I was going to be working in Africa, he looked at me from head to toe and smiled. With my frail physique and thick eyeglasses, I did not look like someone who would embark on a wild Safari adventure any time soon. And I never did. When I came to the continent, I was barely twenty-one years old. While I had my degree and had taken a short course in the French language in France before arriving in Gabon, I was not at all prepared for the life that I was going to live and the challenges that I would encounter. As soon as I arrived, everything seemed different from what I had been accustomed to. After the initial cultural shock, I found my own path to connect with the continent. It was a wild enough ride. I did not need Safari.

This book takes you on a journey of discovery, revelations, magical events, and hilarious—my friends tell me—anecdotes as I have experienced them. This book recounts the journey of how that bespectacled, diminutive, and frail boy survived and even thrived in Africa.

CHAPTER 1

ARRIVAL IN AFRICA

It Was a Dark and Stormy Night – 1979

It was 9:00 p.m. on March 1, 1979. The Swissair flight from Geneva to Libreville was about an hour late. The weather over the skies of Gabon was, as usual, turbulent. The equatorial forests that cover the country generated a constantly humid heat that would rise towards the sky and cause nightly rainstorms with occasional thunder and lightning that sometimes sounded very close and sometimes very far away. This was my first encounter with the continent of Africa.

As the plane approached the runway, some airport lights were totally outshone by the lightning in the sky. After circling the airport a couple of times, the pilot finally decided to land. It was bumpy. The dim runway lights gave glimpses of the dense vegetation that surrounded the airport. The plane reached its parking spot, and the pilot turned off the engines. The gangway that led to the aircraft looked rickety and wobbly. The aircraft door was opened by the crew, and a burst of warm, humid air that smelled of the damp, wild forest started to fill the once-cool cabin. Slowly, the passengers started to disembark.

There was a loud altercation between a passenger and the Swissair crew as we walked over the tarmac towards the terminal, which was a dimly lit, small, short building. The surrounding darkness was so deep that all lights seemed weak and insufficient. There were heavily armed soldiers positioned around the terminal. The disembarked passengers lined up at the open immigration counters. Some medical personnel in white lab coats were walking around, checking the yellow fever vaccination cards of the passengers. There was no air-conditioning in the area, and the heat was becoming intolerable by the minute. The lines moved very slowly.

I noticed the same noisy passenger who was shouting in Arabic, standing outside the two immigration lines. He was dressed in the full Arab thobe, including a head scarf. Somebody came to his side who could translate what he was saying into French. It turned out that he had boarded the wrong flight. His destination was Cairo, Egypt. I felt very sorry for him. But almost immediately, I felt even sorrier for myself because this Arab fellow was going to take another plane and get out of this place very soon.

A couple of my expatriate colleagues were coming to the airport to receive me. I passed through immigration and walked to the luggage delivery area. I waited while everyone picked up their luggage, one by one. Then the carousel stopped, without my bag on it. My colleagues then spotted me, and I told them of my plight. They helped report my missing baggage at the Swissair counter. I was getting more displeased by the minute. I thought that arriving in this strange land without my personal belongings was more than I could take. Luckily, I had some clothes and toiletries in my carry-on bag.

My colleagues took me to my temporary accommodation: an apartment above the bank, which was a small building on the coast of the Atlantic Ocean. Everything in the house felt damp and humid, so I turned on the air conditioner. I went to bed feeling sad for myself. I tried not to think about where I was, but my mind already painted a grim picture. I was alone in this small room on the edge of a dark, menacing forest, alone and unclear of what to expect in the morning. But tiredness overcame me as I pushed those thoughts back and slowly fell asleep. Even during my sleep, I remained aware of the extreme change in my life that had just occurred. I had left the country of my birth and the continent of my ancestors to arrive in an obscure land. Everything seemed different and unfamiliar. How was I going to deal with all this?

... Followed by a lizard-infested but bright morning

When I woke up, the nightly rainstorm had passed, and the sun was shining brightly. I showered and got dressed to go to the bank downstairs. One of my colleagues called to tell me that they had some breakfast for me at the bank. I could go down whenever I was ready.

As I was about to step out of the apartment, I heard a small noise on the balcony. So I went over to check. It was a strange sight. An orange-colored creature that was almost one and a half feet long was lurking on the balcony. I had never seen anything like it. It was some kind of lizard, probably poisonous and deadly. What could I do?

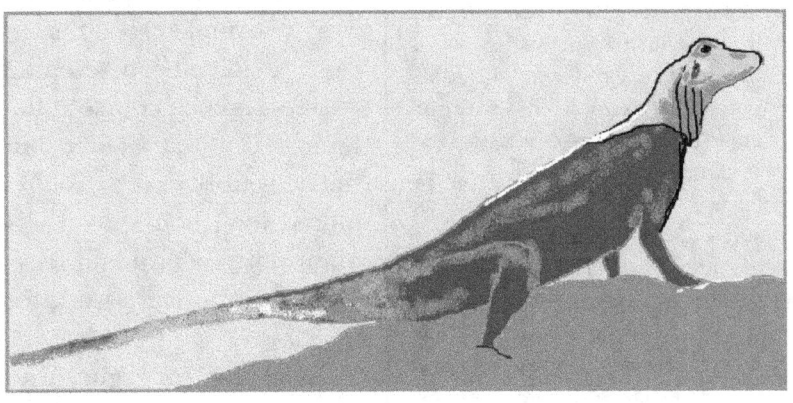

West African Rainbow Lizard (my drawing)

In desperation, I called my colleague to report the sighting of this monster. He did not seem to be concerned at all. He just asked me to leave it alone and go down to the bank. And as I stepped out of the staircase, I immediately knew why my colleague was so calm about the strange lizard. There were literally hundreds of them on the ground in many different colors, shapes, and sizes. They moved to make way as I walked towards the bank entrance.

Starting life in Africa

When I left my home country, I had this false notion that everyone in the world spoke at least some English. This misconception was first shattered in France, where, in 1979, hardly anyone seemed to speak English. Even those who knew some English would not even dare to speak anything other than French. And if I tried to say a few phrases in French, they would react by saying: *"Pardon? Que dites-vous?"* (Excuse me, what did you say?)

By the time I had begun my life in Africa, I had picked up enough French to carry out my day-to-day errands, such as shopping and ordering food in a restaurant.

> The French language thrives on making negative constructions when Standard English has a positive way of expressing the same point. For example, health insurance is called "*assurance maladie*" (sickness insurance). Life insurance is "*assurance décès*" (death assured…). We say in English, "Let's get out of here." The typical French version is: "*Ne restons pas là!*" or "Let's not stay here anymore." The modern French language is indeed trying to change some of these expressions to sound more positive, but this was not the case back then.

However, working in the bank as a department head was a completely different case. I joined an evening business French course at the French Cultural Center, but the daily work in the bank required long hours, so it was often not practical and feasible for me to leave work for the class.

A senior colleague, who was an expat like me and learned French language and literature at the university level, gave me very useful advice. He asked me if I liked to watch movies. I said, "Of course. Everybody likes to watch movies." He then told me to go and watch as many movies in French as I could. There was a decent movie theater near my apartment that premiered a new movie every night. I made a routine of going to my apartment after work, having a quick dinner, and going to the late movie screening.

I watched both French movies and American movies dubbed in French. The only time I didn't go was when I either had dinner plans or the theater was showing a judo-karate or martial arts film. Overall, American movies were easier to follow and understand as the dubbing was in standard French and followed the original English sentence pattern. French movies were much harder to make sense of because of all the slang and unfamiliar sentence patterns.

The lady who sold tickets at the movie theater became accustomed to seeing me almost every night. When I did not show up, the next evening, she would ask where I was the night before.

This nightly movie routine had two visible impacts on me over a few months. First, and more importantly, my French improved dramatically. I stopped worrying about making grammatically correct phrases in my head before speaking. Those phrases would come to me naturally because I had heard them in the movies.

Second, I put on some extra weight. As was the practice in France, this movie theater that I visited frequently also had ice cream on sale during intermission. The ice cream vendors would go through the theater, and almost everyone bought ice cream or potato chips. Popcorn was not yet available in the movie theaters there. Thus, because of my regular visits, my consumption of ice cream started to show on my waistline.

It Began In Africa

Proficiency in French and the waistline growing hand-in-hand

Gabon Circa 1979

Compared to where I came from, Gabon was a very small country. The population number was a sensitive issue. According to a census conducted by the World Bank in 1979, the total population of the country, including foreign workers, was 575,000. However, government authorities insisted that the population of Gabon had crossed one 1 million. The country was run by an autocratic president who had been in power for 12 years and would remain in that position until his death in 2009. He ruled the country for 46 years and handed over the seat to his son, who remained president until he was overthrown by a military coup in 2023.

I was no stranger to autocratic systems of government. In fact, when I left Pakistan, it was governed by a military general who had taken over the reins of power through a military coup. But the two situations were not comparable. Back home, there was a strong opposition to the regime, and there were constant attempts to bring back democratic order. In Gabon, there was no apparent opposition or conflict.

When I lived in Gabon, the country was peaceful and safe. The infrastructure of the city of Libreville was quite good. All utilities (water, power, telephone) worked well. The country enjoyed revenue from petroleum, manganese, uranium, and timber exports. The pharaonic construction of the railway line "Transgabonais" through the equatorial forest was in progress. This railway line connects Libreville to Franceville in the southeast, covering 669 kilometers. It was mainly to be used to transport manganese and uranium from the mines to the port near Libreville.

Most of the businesses were in the hands of foreigners, and even jobs in offices, the port, the railway, the mining, and the petroleum industries were held by them. In the bank where I worked, all departments were headed by foreign nationals except the Department of Human Resources. This department was generally reserved for Gabonese nationals so that they could manage all employment authorizations, work permits, etc.

The French enjoyed a dominant position as owners of larger businesses and industries. There were also many French entrepreneurs who worked as electricians, plumbers, builders, and bar and restaurant owners, to name a few. The Lebanese were also very prominent. They had a strong hold on most trading and import activities. Most shops for consumer goods were owned and managed by Lebanese businessmen. There were also a large number of other African nationals working in Gabon. They were mostly office workers, skilled workers in mining and petroleum, domestic employees, taxi drivers, etc. Some were entrepreneurs involved in small trading and distribution.

Most expatriates were relatively young. Gabon was often the first foreign assignment for many, as it was for me. For the French citizens, it was very easy to arrive and look for a job in Gabon. They could enter the country without a visa; it was not even required to present a passport upon arrival. Their national identity card (even if it was expired) was sufficient to gain entry. Those who were posted by a company to Gabon enjoyed a very comfortable salary and expatriate benefits, including furnished accommodation, a car, and domestic staff. They were entitled to two months of paid vacation and air tickets with family to visit France. Those who came to Gabon in search of work would be hired under a "local hire" contract. The terms of such a contract were not as fabulous as an expat contract, but they were still better than what they would make in a similar position in their home country.

There were also many French advisors, consultants and experts who worked in the government departments on a contractual basis. They would also enjoy two months of annual vacations. Generally speaking, the months of July and August were reserved for such vacations. During those months, if you visited a government ministry, you would notice several offices locked up with signs saying that the occupants were on leave until the end of August.

Government office corridors in Gabon during summer

During the month of August, most government offices were completely deserted. One time, I went to the offices of the Ministry of Commerce and Industry for some paperwork that I needed to accomplish. I thought that I might see the concerned officer in person and manage to obtain the required document. The building of the ministry appeared impressive. It was a U-shaped structure with three floors and a large courtyard. I walked in and first tried to approach reception. It was empty. I tried to look through the corridors to find anybody. There seemed to be no one around. I took the stairs and went to the first floor. Most rooms were shut with signs informing people that they would be here by September, while some were unlocked and empty. I moved to the second floor and walked through the corridors. At one point, I could hear sounds from a distance. It seemed that there were some people present on that floor, after all.

I followed in the direction of the voices and reached a conference hall. About twenty staff members were gathered in that room in front of a television. Football. I tried to grab their attention, but they were not interested. One person signaled me to come in and watch the game with them. I do enjoy watching sports, including football, but I arrived in that building during my work hours for a specific professional reason. I could not sit down and watch the game. There was no chance that I would find the right individual in this crowd of football fans who would know about my file. I waited for a while and left the scene.

CHAPTER 2

THE WORDS GET IN THE WAY

(Mis)Communication in Africa – 1980

I began to work under a boss who left an everlasting impression on me. Although he had so many exceptional traits, I want to focus on his linguistic genius. He had an unbelievable gift. He could massacre every language that he spoke. He came from the same ethnic background as I do, so we either spoke in Urdu or English. However, he would boldly converse in French with the staff and the customers even though he was strongly advised to use a translator when talking to people like clients, auditors, lawyers, or regulators. When he did use a translator, it was

> **Languages of Africa**
> The number of languages natively spoken in Africa is estimated to be between 1,250 and 2,100. Nigeria alone has over 500 languages. The largest language families in Africa are Niger-Congo, Afroasiatic, and Austronesian.
>
> The Niger-Congo family is spoken by over **700 million** people across the continent, making it the **largest** language family in Africa and one of the **largest** in the world. It includes languages such as Swahili, Yoruba, Igbo, and Zulu. The Afroasiatic family, on the other hand, is spoken by over **500 million** people across West Asia, North Africa, the Horn of Africa, and parts of the Sahara and Sahel. It includes languages such as Arabic, Amharic, and Hausa.

It Began In Africa

> The Niger-Congo family is further divided into several subfamilies, including the Bantu, Mande, and Kordofanian subfamilies. The Bantu subfamily is the **largest** subfamily of the Niger-Congo family and includes over **500 languages** spoken in Central, East, and Southern Africa. The Afroasiatic family is divided into six branches: Berber, Chadic, Cushitic, Egyptian, Semitic, and Omotic. Arabic, if counted as a single language, is by far the most widely spoken within the family, with around **300 million** native speakers concentrated primarily in the Middle East and North Africa.

> Here is an overview of the major language families and linguistic landscape of Africa:
> - **Niger-Congo language family:** The largest language family in Africa in terms of number of speakers. It includes Bantu languages spoken across much of sub-Saharan Africa, as well as many languages in West Africa like Yoruba, Igbo, Ewe, etc.
> - **Afroasiatic languages:** This family includes languages like Arabic, Somali, Amharic, Hausa, and others spoken across North Africa, the Horn of Africa, parts of West Africa, and parts of East Africa.
> - **Nilo-Saharan languages:** Languages centered around the

often a challenge for the translators themselves.

In addition to the linguistic sabotage, he was also a master in the mispronunciation of proper names. His secretary was a very cheerful and rather bubbly French lady named Renée, whose name was pronounced by the boss as "Reno." This was very close to the name of the French car brand, Renault. One day, he came out of his office, looking for his secretary. He saw a junior accounting clerk walking by and asked him where "Reno" was. The young clerk replied, "With Shadrack." Shadrack was a bank driver. He often drove a Renault, a vehicle in the bank's carpool. Shadrack was a short and bulky fellow from Nigeria. He belonged to the Igbo community that settled in Gabon after the Biafra Civil War in Nigeria. He spoke a colorful, Pidgin-flavored English that was well worth listening to.

The boss was surprised to hear this answer. He demanded, "Why would Reno be with Shadrack?" accompanied by an intimidating tone. The young man replied meekly, "Sir, Shadrack says that he is the only one who can handle Reno." By this time, the boss was in full rage. "What?" he shouted. "How can you say such a thing?" The poor clerk was now completely shaken by the direction this conversation was going. He had no idea why the boss would be so upset to learn that a bank driver was driving the bank's old Renault-18. He tried to save his own skin and explained, "Sir, everyone knows that. Shadrack takes the Renault almost every day."

This was the last straw. The boss screamed out the name of the chief administration officer, who was the ultimate boss of both the driver and this young clerk. The chief officer happened to be nearby, and on hearing his name being screamed out in the corridor, he appeared immediately. At this point, an audience was growing around them. Each listener was probably making their own picture of what was going on. The idea of this Shadrack fellow in his driver's uniform stealing away the boss' very sophisticated and fancy secretary every day for joy rides or who knows what was as incredible as it was hilarious.

---

upper parts of the Nile River in eastern and north central Africa, including Maasai, Songhai, Fur, and Kanuri.

- **Khoisan languages:** Typified by the use of click consonants, these languages are centered in southern Africa and include Nama, Khwe, and the San languages.
- **Austronesian languages:** Spoken in Madagascar, these languages, like Malagasy, arrived from seafaring people from Southeast Asia.

Additionally, there are:

- **Creole languages** in West Africa and islands off the west coast that blended African and European languages
- **Unclassified languages** in parts of Africa, like the Laal language in Chad and Jalaa in Nigeria, that may be linguistic isolates unconnected to other families
- Sign languages emerging in deaf communities across Africa
- Languages brought from colonial influences like English, French, Spanish, Portuguese, and others in many parts of Africa

It Began In Africa

Africa has a highly diverse linguistic landscape, with several major African language families spoken alongside languages rooted in colonial and migratory impacts. Many multilingual countries feature languages from multiple families.

Colonial Legacy Languages:

Africans are, in most cases, multilingual. They speak several of their native languages and often speak one of the European languages that remains the official language of their country. European and other non-African languages have a presence in many parts of Africa due to colonization, migration, and globalization:

- **English:** Spoken widely in former British colonies like Nigeria, Kenya, and Uganda, and more as an official language, such as lingua franca.
- **French:** Used extensively in former French and Belgian colonies across North, West, and Central Africa, as well as Indian Ocean islands. Countries like Senegal, Congo, and Chad use French.
- **Portuguese:** Angola, Mozambique, Guinea-Bissau, Cape Verde and Sao Tome and Principe speak Portuguese post-colonization.
- **Spanish:** Equatorial Guinea and parts of Morocco/Western Sahara speak Spanish from colonization history.

The boss was furious beyond imagination.

But all good things must come to an end. Some killjoy, know-it-all lady from the customer service department walked in and ruined the drama. She asked the boss to calm down. She then announced that the poor clerk was under the impression that the boss was asking about Renault, the automobile brand. However, the boss was certainly asking about the whereabouts of his secretary, Renée. What followed was a couple of giggles first and then a huge collective laughter. The boss himself caught on last—his secretary was not eloping with his driver, after all. The exact cause of the misunderstanding was still elusive to him, but by now, his anger was replaced by an uncomfortable smile. He shook his head and stepped back into his office, leaving the audience to continue to enjoy the classic comedy that their boss unwittingly provided them from time to time. A couple of days later, Shadrack mentioned to me that everybody smiles at him now. "Do I look that funny?" he asks. I could not tell him the story, so I just pretended that I had no idea. It must be his charming personality.

I worked under this boss for just two years, but the stories of this period have remained with me forever, most of them involving his mishandling of French.

One day, he received tragic news. One of his relatives had died in an air crash in Saudi Arabia. He was devastated to hear this, and he went home right away. At the end of the workday, I joined several other colleagues to visit him at his house to offer our condolences. We found him in his living room, wearing a dressing gown, nesting an alcoholic beverage in his hands. By his demeanor, it was obvious that he had been drinking the stuff the whole afternoon. He listened to our words of condolence and shook his head in sorrow.

After an awkward pause, he said in a philosophical tone, "The man, he don't know. Today, he is dead; to-

Languages that arrived in Africa due to large-scale population movements:
- **Arabic:** The expansion of Islam and trade networks helped Arabic languages spread across North Africa and the Horn of Africa over the centuries.
- **Malagasy:** The language of Madagascar reflects the influence of Southeast Asian Austronesian settlers.

Expat/Settler Community Languages:
- English is also spoken by British and other expats in countries like Egypt, Zambia, Zimbabwe and South Africa
- French settler populations exist in North and West Africa
- Chinese and Indian languages are used among trader/business communities in places like Nigeria and Kenya.

So, while Africa is dominated by its indigenous languages, global geopolitics and migration flows have added European/foreign languages into Africa's rich linguistic tapestry today. These languages co-exist in a multilingual landscape alongside native African tongues.

LANGUAGES THAT STAND APART

I have specially chosen to mention certain languages in the description below due to some very unique aspects that are worth noting.

It Began In Africa

> **Languages with clicks**
>
> Spoken by tribes scattered across the southern parts of Africa, the Khoisan languages may not be widespread, but they more than make up for it in personality. They are the rebels of the African linguistic landscape, flouting phonetic norms with their creative repertoire of attention-grabbing click sounds. Where most languages are content with the mundane old options of sounding out words with A, B, C, and the rest of the humdrum alphabet gang, Khoisan laughs in their boring faces. These languages said, "We're doing things our way, with pop, smack, and clickity-clack explosions of sound that will leave your jaw unhinged!"
>
> Speakers have no hope of keeping a stiff upper lip when chatting in tongues like Nama with its trifecta of clunky clicks made by razzing the side of the cheek, touching the roof of the mouth or clucking at the back of the throat. Conversations sound like a frenzied session of tongue twisters with all the ! and @ symbols flying around!

morrow, he is alive." Despite the somber occasion, his very sad face, the dim atmosphere of his living room and the deep philosophical tone of his voice, it was hard for us to control our reaction. One of my colleagues, who was from India, sitting next to me, could not resist whispering in my ear, "Our boss is referring to the reincarnation theory."

Whatever my boss lacked in language and communication expertise, he more than made up in his confidence, audacity, boldness, and dedication to achieve results. But he had very little regard for the people he managed, especially the expatriate staff who ran everything in the bank. He would withhold their privileges, make them work extremely long hours, including weekends, and would not acknowledge their contributions nor report about it to the head office.

I recall one classic example. He wrote a memo to his direct boss in London about the annual results of the bank in Gabon, declaring that he had "single-handedly" achieved such heights of performance. The irony of this story was that the memo itself was drafted by a senior colleague who served as his official scribe, so to speak because he could not write straight English or any other language.

I found his overreaching personality and despotic behavior completely unacceptable from the first week I began working with him, but I also noted that all the other colleagues, while they complained a lot, were completely resigned to their fates and would not do anything about it. There was not much that I could do to improve the situation. I was barely twenty-two years old at that time. Though I was fascinated by the country and the continent, the work environment seemed too toxic.

After some thinking, I wrote my resignation letter and went to his office to deliver it to him. But before I could broach the subject of my resignation, he started on a work-related issue. He told me that the junior officers must work on the weekends to cover the backlog and other things like past-due reconciliations. The fact was that we did work on all Saturdays but the previous Saturday because

But don't assume that the Khoisan crew doesn't take their linguistics seriously just because they pepper words with cheeky clicks that stir up a ruckus. These quirky languages know how to be the life of the grammar party while still being as complex as the strictest syllable sultan.

So next time you listen to the San and their fellow click-clack Khoisan kith and kin chatter, remember: even if you can't join their conversation, you can still appreciate those fabulous phonetic firecrackers!

Lingala of Congo

I have been fascinated by the melodious and rhythmic sounds of Lingala. Lingala is a Bantu language that developed as a lingua franca along the Congo River during the late nineteenth century. It is now spoken by over 45 million people across the northern Democratic Republic of Congo, as well as regions of Angola, the Central African Republic and the Republic of Congo.

As a language that emerged from contact and trade between different ethnic groups like the Bobangi, Bangala, Mabalia, and Libinza, Lingala has a diverse vocabulary that draws from multiple source languages. It absorbed words from African languages like Kikongo as well as from European languages we were invited to a cultural event that we all went to see in the afternoon. I told him that everyone was working very hard and that he must appreciate their efforts. He looked at me and spoke in a low voice of authority, "Listen, you have to follow as I tell you. Otherwise, you have no place in this organization. I am the absolute power in Gabon."

I found his last sentence hilarious. Not even the dictator president of Gabon would make such a claim openly. Keeping my voice even lower than him, I took out my resignation letter from my pocket and put it on his table, telling him, "Yes, I agree that this is not the place for me. That is why I am submitting my resignation." He did not fully follow what was going on at first. He put his reading glasses on and looked at the paper on his desk. He could not believe what he read. How could I resign like this? How could I anticipate the conversation and have the resignation letter ready in my pocket? He was in total shock. He told me that he could not accept it.

I replied that I knew the rules. In the case of a resignation of expatriate staff, he was supposed to forward it to the head office in London with his remarks for a final decision. This was

---

> like French and Portuguese during the colonial era.
>
> Lingala first served as a common means of communication along the river trade routes, and its use expanded with the migration of Congolese people. It was first used by Catholic missionaries to spread the faith in the army and education circles. This led to Lingala becoming one of DRC's four designated national languages post-independence.
>
> Today, Lingala's core region of speakers is found in the northwestern part of DRC, including major cities like Kinshasa and Kisangani, where it is widely spoken alongside French. Through much of the twentieth century, a standardized dialect of Lingala emerged based on the Kinshasa speech patterns. Contemporary Lingala displays influences from French while retaining its rich Bantu language base that bridges diverse Congolese ethnic groups. Both linguistic research and popular music continue to sustain Lingala's vitality as a language today.

even more disturbing for him to hear. I was challenging his authority just a few minutes after his declaration that he was the absolute power in the country.

The matter was escalated further as other junior colleagues joined me in a collective resignation move in the coming days. This turn of events broke his reign of terror that he had enjoyed since before my arrival, in about 4 years. In a compromise suggested by some senior colleagues, the boss agreed to tone down his attitude and pressure tactics. He agreed to change his ways and allowed for a more reasonable working environment.

Having recounted these stories, I am not trying to place the blame for all miscommunication on the African continent solely on my ex-boss. He certainly played an important role, but Africa is huge and linguistically diverse.

Take, for instance, these short anecdotes from the community of English speakers from the Biafra Region of Nigeria, like the Shadrack

---

Lingala has some very interesting tonal and rhyming qualities as part of its verbal artistry. One major feature that contributes to its lyrical nature is alliterative word pairs, where two linked words start with the same letter or sound. Some examples of these alliterative couplings common in Lingala include:

- Lekoléla – meaning "it shines intensely"
- Bokatála – for "break/cause damage"
- Yákoyéteka – "walk with a limp"
- Tokólota – "flow/overflow"

The repetition creates a catchy sing-song rhythm within phrases. In terms of rhyme schemes, Lingala lyrics often employ rhyming doublet structures linking two syllables together, such as:

- Ngái ngái
- Lengé lengé
- Toba toba

Not only does this set up a pleasing rhyme but also rhythm, as the second doubled word is stressed more than the first. Songs will incorporate clever plays on such couplet rhymes as musical motifs that aurally resonate for the listener.

Overall, from the alliterative pairings to the rhyme doublets, there are strong poetic and musical qualities embedded directly with-

It Began In Africa

in Lingala's vocabulary and phonetics. Speakers can deftly weave these linguistic elements together to achieve rhyme, wordplay and vocal harmonies that give Lingala its distinctly lyrical flavor. From folk songs to pop hits, these rhyming linguistic devices serve as the building blocks of harmony underpinning Lingala's verbal art.

Yoruba language
Yoruba is a tonal language belonging to the Niger-Congo family and native to West Africa. It is spoken by over 30 million people, mainly across Nigeria and Benin, with speaker populations in other nearby countries like Togo and Sierra Leone as well.

As Nigeria's second most spoken tongue after Hausa, Yoruba serves as a major language in the southern regions of the country. It bears some linguistic similarity to other languages like Igala and Idoma further north in Central Nigeria.

The Yoruba language is characterized by its three-tone system, alternating between high, mid, and low pitches to convey lexical differences in an agglutinative manner. This tonal quality gives Yoruba spoken poetry and lyrics a distinctive melodic nature and rhythmic quality.

In its syllable structure, consonant and vowel combinations can be quite complex compared to West-

fellow, who settled in Gabon. The Igbos, as they are called, arrived in Gabon during the secessionist conflict in Nigeria, known as the Biafran Civil War. It was a brutal conflict that took place from 1967 to 1970. The southeastern provinces of Nigeria rebelled against the central government and claimed independence. The rebels were supported by France and its allies in Africa, including the president of Gabon, who accepted a number of war refugees from the zone to settle in the country. The Igbo community was mostly traders, many of them specializing in automobile spare parts.

They were natural clients of our bank because of the language. Most of our staff were bilingual, and we could do all our business in English. It was a real pleasure to hear them talk, for they spoke a very colorful language that was filled with their native Pidgin expressions. When they wrote to the bank, they had a tendency to be hyperbolic and long-winded. Their spoken language was even more entertaining. For instance, I asked one of them in the bank: "How are you?" His reply was: "Beautiful like a horse." (To this day, I am not sure where this comes from. I heard this expression a few times.) I also heard this conversation between two customers from this community who were just chatting in the bank: "I went to visit you in your shop, but you offered me no tea." The answer was short and grim, "You know, water never hot."

I recall a letter that one of these customers had written to complain about a credit report that the bank gave about their company. Apparently, the account had a small balance and had registered no transactions in a long time. The letter began with this poetic line: "Brick by brick, the house was built and also no smoking without fire." The point they were trying to make was that they were building their business gradually. But there had never been an incident, such as a bounced check, on their account.

Many years later, I watched an episode of *Star Trek: The Next Generation* called "Darmok." The alien species in this story spoke in allegories. This reminded me of some of the expressions that I had heard from the Igbo people in Gabon.

---

ern languages—syllables like gb, ewu, gbe and ogun display combinations less common outside Africa.

The Yoruba people historically lived in city-states and kingdoms before the European colonization. The language has many loanwords absorbed into its vocabulary from historical Portuguese, French, and English contact. Yoruba also bears traces of Arabic influence.

Today, Yoruba vocabulary and speech display stylistic variation across Nigeria's diverse regions. Contemporary works of Yoruba theater, fiction, poetry, and hip-hop continue to breathe new vitality into the language and sustain its rich identity. Traditional Yoruba religion also offers a well of spirituality expressed through this historical West African tongue.

CHAPTER 3

COLD WAR AND AFRICA

Financing of Proxy Battles on the Continent – 1980

When I arrived in Africa in 1979, the world was solidly divided into the Eastern and Western blocs. Every conflict on the planet was connected to this divide. While the Vietnam War ended in 1975, two civil wars were raging in Africa in two ex-colonies of Portugal, namely, Angola and Mozambique. Various political groups had fought against the colonial power to gain independence of Angola in 1975, but immediately after independence, war broke out between the pro-Soviet group People's Movement for Liberation of Angola (MPLA) and the pro-West National Union for Total Independence of Angola (UNITA).

A similar situation occurred in Mozambique. The civil war began in 1977, a couple of years after its independence. The ruling party, FRELIMO, was opposed by RENAMO and supported by a bunch of smaller groups like UNAMO, COREMO, UNIPOMO, and FUMO. As was the case in Angola, the ruling FRELIMO was supported by the Soviet bloc, whereas the RENAMO had the backing of South Africa, Rhodesia (Zimbabwe today), and Western countries. Some countries in Africa were openly supporting the leftist groups in these two countries. They had the moral cover of the erstwhile Organization for African Unity (now African Union) and the Non-Aligned Movement. Some other countries were on the side of the Western-backed factions in those wars. They kept a very low profile and never publicly showed their support for UNITA in Angola or RENAMO in Mozambique.

All of this was very far away from my place of posting in Africa, and I would not have anything to do with it except for the fact that Gabon was one of those countries that had chosen to assist the West in their proxy wars in Angola and Mozambique. I had the opportunity to witness that first-hand during my first year in Gabon. I was in charge of the cash and customer deposits department of the bank. It was a stressful assignment as I carried the keys to the coffers of the bank. I supervised a group of cashiers who were older and far more experienced than me. So, I had to be on my toes all the time. Otherwise, they could cause deliberate cash shortages that would become a responsibility.

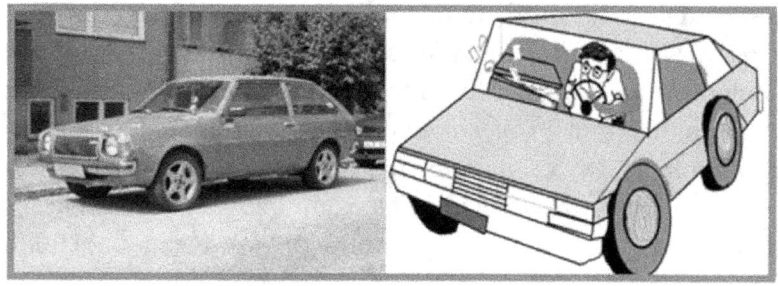

Mazda 323 circa 1978

One morning, when I had just finished opening the cash counters of the bank, the general manager's secretary came to tell me that I had to go to the presidential palace to collect a certain amount of US dollars from the president himself. I had never had such an assignment before. I tried to ask other colleagues about it. Nobody knew much about it, and it seemed that the manager had handled such operations himself in the past. But now he had asked me, through his secretary, to do it. On the one hand, it was a sign of his trust in me. On the other hand, I was a twenty-two-year-old, rather small, young man with thick spectacles, a shy demeanor, and a Mazda 323.

The secretary taught me how to get to the presidential palace, and I, very reluctantly, drove myself there. The entrance was heavily guarded by armed soldiers who did not look friendly at all. They actually appeared hostile. As instructed, I told them that I had an appointment with the president's personal secretary, Mrs. Carpentier. When I gave this name, they slowed down and took another look at me. They had discussions among themselves that I could not follow.

Then, one of the soldiers, who looked like their senior, picked up one of the phones on his desk and made a call. The call was very short and ended abruptly. He then signaled one of the soldiers, who quickly approached me. I had no idea what was going on. I was almost certain that this soldier was coming to arrest me or something of that sort. I was very worried.

The senior soldier told me to follow this other soldier. I had no choice. Did I mention that they were heavily armed? I followed him into the building, and after riding the elevator and going up a flight of stairs, I arrived at an office. It was the office of the secretary, Mrs. Carpentier. She turned out to be a very nice lady. She was originally from Mauritius. She told me that the president was waiting for me. Yes, the president of the republic, the ultimate boss and the head honcho of the entire country of Gabon, was waiting for me! This had never happened before. Again, my feelings of deep exhilaration were hindered by deeper apprehension.

Mrs. Carpentier pointed towards a large door and asked me to go in. And I did. It was a huge room. The lighting was rather dim. I could see statues, decorative masks, flags, stuffed eagles, and, on one side, an oversized desk. Behind the desk was an oversized portrait of the president. Right next to the desk stood a diminutive man wearing a green cape. As I approached the desk, he turned towards me, greeted me, and shook my hand. He had a very warm smile and glowing eyes.

Without further ado, he said that he had received some money for Angola. But there was no immediate transportation available, so I could take these funds and keep them for him. If he needed to convert them into local currency, he would ask us. Otherwise, he would ask for the same dollars back. This was not practical from my bank's point of view. We were obliged to account for the incoming money. We could not just take them for safekeeping.

At this point, my banking reflexes came back. I explained to him that we could convert them into local currency right away. Whenever he needed the dollars, we would arrange for them within three working days. He liked the idea. He said it was fine with him. Please convert them and bring me the CFA francs (the local currency). At this point, he pushed a button on his desk, and the wall behind his desk, including his oversized portrait, slid open. I almost lost my breath, not because of the sliding wall but because of what I saw in that closet.

The closet was full of guns of all shapes and sizes, a formidable collection of automatic rifles, machine guns, bazookas, and all. Ignoring the collection of armaments, and very nonchalantly, he picked up a suitcase from the closet and shut it back. Once he opened the case, I saw stacks of $100 bills. He told me that they were already counted. The total was $1.6 million. He shut the suitcase again and handed it to me. I picked up the suitcase and unceremoniously walked out of this strange office.

Outside, the secretary was waiting for me. She asked me to sign in a little notebook, which confirmed that, apparently, I had received a file of documents. I said goodbye to Mrs. Carpentier. She asked another guard to show me out. I went back through the same route that I had taken earlier, but this time, with the suitcase full of dollars, it seemed much longer. What if this guard snatches the bag away from me? However, nothing of the sort occurred, and I arrived at the palace's exit.

The soldiers looked suspiciously at my suitcase but did not say a word. I walked towards my car, which was parked on the other side of the street. This was one of the most fearsome walks I ever took. I reached my car and put the suitcase in the trunk, but almost immediately, I had a change of mind. I placed the bag next to me in the front seat and drove to the bank. It was a very short drive, but it seemed like it would never end with the traffic lights. I arrived safely at the bank and sat down in my boss's office to debrief.

After my first stressful but successful collection of the war chest, my bosses thought that I was a natural for such assignments. I tried to explain that I had never been more shaken and frightened in my short life, but they ignored my complaints.

So, I was often assigned similar tasks. Sometimes, we would receive US dollars against the local currency, and sometimes, we were asked to produce US dollars against the local currency. We would keep the US dollars for a couple of weeks, but under the currency exposure rules, we had to dispose of them. When we were obligated to do so, we informed our valued clients that we had disposed of them, and if they required the dollars again, we would need to order them from our correspondent bank in Europe.

On one of those occasions when we were asked to deliver US dollars, the order was placed, and the delivery date was set up to five days due to the bank holidays in France. Our esteemed client was not happy with this long lead time and had called repeatedly about it. In those days, funds were transported through a regular airfreight on a scheduled flight. The captain of the plane would carry the funds under his direct control and deliver them to the designated person upon arrival.

When I had to take such a delivery, I would show up at the airport when the flight arrived with a Telex airway bill, see the captain in person, and he would deliver the bag of dollars

It Began In Africa

to me against a signed receipt. The process was quick and unceremonious.

On this particular occasion, when I arrived at the airport, I noticed that the UTA(Union de Transports Aeriens, a now-defunct French airline) plane was already on the tarmac. The flight had arrived earlier than the scheduled time. I rushed to the airline counters and asked to see the captain of the arriving flight. They said that he was not around. I explained to them that I was there to collect a package that the captain was carrying for my bank. Nobody seemed to have a clue.

I was getting concerned about the situation when I noticed a flight attendant in the UTA uniform that must have been on the incoming flight. I approached her and asked if she knew where the pilot of the flight was. She pointed towards the bar. She said that he was having a drink there while waiting for the crew, who would fly the plane back to Paris later in the evening. The captain was with his copilot, and they were enjoying tall glasses of the local beer. It was called Regab which signified "régaler les gabonais"(to please the Gabonese).

I greeted them and showed him my piece of paper for the delivery. He looked at it and told me that I was not to worry. Another person had already taken the delivery. At that point, I felt like I was hit by a bullet. What? Someone else had taken the delivery of the dollars? How? He was not perturbed. He said that he was told by the local customs officers that it was okay to deliver the bag to that gentleman. Who was that gentleman? The captain did not have a clue and did not seem to care. He had done his job of carrying the package and delivering it upon arrival. He even complained that it was quite stressful to carry such packages. Even when he had to go to the washroom on the plane, he was worried that his copilot would steal it. This last sentence was supposed to be a joke, and both he and the copilot laughed and raised their glasses towards me. The captain offered me a drink. "Thanks, but no thanks," was my answer.

I was in a total panic mode by then. In a desperate attempt to find out what had happened, I asked the captain if he had the name of the person who took the delivery. He replied that it must be on the receipt. I begged him to at least show me that receipt. He seemed fine with that. He dug into his pilot's briefcase and came up with the green color airway bill copy with the handwritten receipt. The name of the recipient was written in broken handwriting, but I could make out that it was a certain Colonel Cazeneuve. Who was this person? A French army colonel.

I was trying to think fast. My mind was telling me that I had been scammed by the French mafia. The 1971 thriller film *The French Connection* kept popping up in my mind. I imagined that someone in their circles had received the information about the incoming package of dollars and had arranged an easy pickup. I left the pilots in the bar and walked out towards my car. I thought that the mafia had sent a person dressed as a fake colonel with a fake name, like Cazeneuve, to impress the airline pilot and recover the bag without much effort.

I had to immediately update both my bank and the office of the president. The lack of cell phones at the time was the cause of so much hardship and misery in those days, and nobody seemed to notice it. My assignment was to collect the package and head straight to the presidential palace, where I would deliver it to Mrs. Carpentier, the president's personal assistant. This time, however, I had to go to her empty-handed and explain what happened. I was wondering whether I should stop at the bank first to break the terrifying news of the stolen dollars or head straight to the palace.

There was a strong chance that I would be taken into custody by the presidential guards for investigation. However, I did not want to delay communication with the office of the president by stopping at the bank where my seniors would want me to sit down and make a written report. So, I left the airport in my little car with big worries in my head. I did not foresee any positive outcome. Some people had taken the dollars, but the president would not pay for them. He would be unhappy that we could not deliver as promised. The bank had already paid for the dollars, and I was assigned to collect them. I had failed in doing so while a certain Colonel named Cazeneuve had succeeded in taking the money and running (probably, as the song goes, to Venezuela).

I arrived at the presidential palace, sweating and nervous after a twenty-minute drive. I was now known to the guards at the entrance. I asked to see Mrs. Carpentier and was ushered into the building. I went straight to her office. She looked at my panicked face and asked me what was going on. I told her the story as quickly as I could. When I reached the part where a member of the French Mafia, dressed as an army colonel, probably looking like the French actor Jean-Paul Belmondo, stole the dollars, she could not control her laughter.

Now, I had completely lost track of what was going on. I was expecting shock and disbelief, followed by anger. I was dreading the part where she would send me to the office of the president to tell the story to him. But she seemed relaxed and amused.

She told me not to worry. This is exactly what the captain had said. It had not reduced my worries. She asked me again to relax because the package had been collected by the military attaché of the president, a certain Colonel Cazeneuve, in person. This was done because the president's office had been informed of the early arrival of the aircraft, and the president had, therefore, sent his man to collect the funds.

"How could he do it?" I asked. "The funds were ordered by the bank and were sent in the name of the bank!" Mrs. Carpentier responded, "Because he is the boss!" The person to whom the president was supposed to hand over the dollars had already arrived. So, being the boss, he decided to cut to the chase and get the package picked up directly.

The relief at this turn of the story was deep and revitalizing. I stopped sweating and began to feel how cold the room was with the air conditioning running full blast. I realized what had happened, and my banking brain started to recognize all the irregularities in this scenario from a procedural viewpoint. The funds had gone directly from the pilot to the president without the usual passage through the banking channel.

To remedy this, I needed proof of the president's receipt of funds to allow the bank to register the transaction. I told that to Mrs. Carpentier. She asked me to have a seat and prepare a receipt. She would type it on a paper, and then I could go to the president's office to get his signature. I had to face him after all, but in better circumstances than I had feared earlier.

I wrote down the receipt, and she typed it on a paper. She inserted the paper in a folder and spoke with the president on the phone. He instructed her that I may be shown in right away. Under normal circumstances, I would have felt awkward and uncomfortable at these encounters, but with the rollercoaster ride that I had been through that day, I felt very relaxed about facing the president. As I walked into that office with its stuffed birds and statues, I had a feeling that there was no one else in there. I looked all around. Not a soul.

While I was trying to decide whether to sit down somewhere to wait or just keep standing, a bookshelf on one side of the room slid open like in a James Bond movie. The president walked through that entrance, and when he had fully entered the room, the bookshelf slid back to shut the entry point. He seemed to be in good spirits, too. He smiled and told me that he had the package picked up from the airport.

I smiled back and handed him the receipt for his signature. He laughed and asked, "Why should I sign it? You did not deliver anything to me." I was going to have another panic attack before he picked up a golden fountain pen from his desk, affixed his bold and very familiar signature on the paper, and handed it back to me. He shook my hand and said he was pleased with our bank's service.

Jonas Savimbi – Angolan war lord (my drawing)

Obviously, the funds that he had ordered were meant to finance the ongoing civil war in Angola. The proxy war between the Western and Soviet Bloc that was being fought between the ruling MPLA headed by Eduardo dos Santos and the rebellion group UNITA run by Jonas Savimbi went on until 2002 with brief interludes of peace.

Meanwhile, the Berlin Wall fell in November 1989, and the Soviet backing for the ruling group MPLA came to a halt. This gave the rebel leader of UNITA false hope for an impending victory. He was counting on the continued support from the West, but he was mistaken. The Western assistance was not going to continue. The political change in South Africa and the fall of the Soviet Union had removed all the reasons that would justify continued support to a rebel group in Angola that had not been successful in spite of all the money and material support. In fact, the entire southern African region had clearly rallied behind Eduardo dos Santos. Savimbi's friends advised him to reach a peace settlement and put an end to the civil war. There were several attempts, with the help of international diplomacy, to reach a compromise. However, Savimbi remained combative and defiant in spite of large-scale defections from his political and military structure.

His location had always been kept secret, but according to some stories, he made a mobile phone call to his daughter in Côte d'Ivoire, which was detected by a Western intelligence agency that leaked it to the Angolan authorities. Armed with this vital information, they sent a strong contingent to the leaked location. A fierce battle ensued, and Savimbi died in that ambush on February 22, 2002. His death stopped all fighting, and the country has been at peace since then.

CHAPTER 4

RELICS OF THE COLONIAL ERA

4.1 A Visit to Dr. Schweitzer's Hospital, Lambarene, Gabon – 1981

Gabon is full of mysteries. Some of them are related to the locations that tell stories of the arrival of Europeans, their interactions with the native populations, and how they tried to survive and establish themselves. But the story of Dr. Albert Schweitzer is probably the most unique. He was an accomplished musician, physicist, mathematician, theologian, and medical doctor from Alsace, a region that was, until the end of World War I, a part of Germany. After the war, the region was annexed to France.

Albert Schweitzer decided to abandon his very sophisticated social, cultural, and professional life and move to equatorial Africa. He chose the area of Lambarene because it was accessible by boat through the Ogoué River from Port-Gentil on the Atlantic coast. The location was a dense equatorial forest. The medical and religious communities in Europe were aware of the endemic tropical diseases, particularly a growing number of cases of leprosy, in that region, and a Catholic mission was already doing some relief work there.

It Began In Africa

Dr. Schweitzer and his wife arrived in Lambarene for the first time in 1912. He set up a small medical facility with the support of the church mission and worked in extremely tough conditions. Gradually, he set up his makeshift hospital and treated thousands of patients. By 1914, World War I had broken out in Europe. He was a German citizen living in a French colony. His movements were restricted by the French authorities, and in 1917, he was deported to France, where he was arrested for several months. When the Great War ended in 1918, he was freed and became a French citizen.

After recovering from illnesses related to his imprisonment, he began his project to return to Africa with all the required provisions and equipment that he could collect and carry. It took him a while to be fully prepared, based on his earlier experience on the ground. He returned to Lambarene in 1924 with his wife and a team of medical workers. Others followed him later from different parts of Europe. He set up a much more elaborate medical and surgical facility on the site.

He continued to expand and develop the process for the coming years. He made several trips back to Europe, and gradually, his work in Africa became known all over the world. He received the Nobel Prize for Peace in 1952 for his heroic achievements in providing healthcare in the heart of Africa. He died in 1965 in Lambarene.

This rather lengthy introduction was necessary, I assure you. My story takes place in 1981. As I was working at the bank in Libreville, Gabon, I noticed that one elderly British lady used to visit the bank once a month to collect a transfer from London. It was not a usual occurrence, and as such, I was curious about this person.

During one of her visits, I happened to be sitting at the desk that handled the payment of her transfer. While completing the paperwork, I took the initiative to ask her what her occupation was. She told me that she lived and worked in Dr. Schweitzer's Hospital in Lambarene. The transfer of a modest amount that she received every month was a pension paid to her by the British government.

Her answer raised more questions in my mind. I asked her if she would like to have a cup of tea to talk to me about Lambarene. I thought a British person would not refuse a cup of tea. But she flatly refused. She said she did not mind telling me about Lambarene, but she had stopped drinking tea a very long time ago. In fact, she had stopped eating any solid foods for several years. She only drank milk. I was completely taken aback by what she said. I thought that she was just trying to appear mysterious. Containing my disbelief, I played along and asked several questions about the hospital, her role and how she got there.

She arrived in Lambarene more than 25 years ago. This was before Gabon was established as a French colony. She worked with Dr. Schweitzer, initially as a nurse and later in various positions, for about ten years. After his death, she continued to carry on her work. Naturally, I asked her about the circumstances that brought her to Lambarene from England. Her answer was emotional. She explained that she had been married to a British army officer for just one year when he died in an accident. This was a life-shattering event for her.

After a short period of grief and depression, she decided to devote the rest of her life to a heroic cause in memory of her late husband. She was a trained nurse and had heard about Dr. Schweitzer's work. In a rush of emotions and selflessness, she decided to join Dr. Schweitzer in Africa and assist him in his work. With minimal provisions, including some detailed maps, she made this journey of devotion not by ship but through land and on foot.

She arrived on the continent from Spain and traveled through Morocco, Algeria, Niger, Nigeria, and Cameroon and finally reached Gabon. It took her several months and much suffering. The news of her journey had already reached Lambarene. In advance of her journey, she had sent a letter to

Dr. Schweitzer. She very quickly settled there and began to work under the Grand Doctor.

Dr. Albert Schweitzer (my drawing)

She had turned out to be a great storyteller. I forgot about the work that was piling on my desk. She continued to tell me about her experiences. I was heartbroken to hear about the challenges she faced in her mission to bring healthcare to the most downtrodden and isolated people in the world. To add to her miseries, Dr. Schweitzer was a very tough boss. He ruled over the hospital village as a despot in many ways. She learned to live and work under those circumstances.

When it was finally her time to leave and go back to Lambarene, she invited me to come and visit the hospital with my friends and colleagues, and she would be happy to show us around. Among the most unbelievable things that she told me was the fact that she came to Libreville from Lambarene every month or so on foot. Yes, leisurely walking 240 kilometers back and forth. I told this story to my colleagues and friends. They were fascinated. Everyone wanted to visit the hospital and speak to this lady who only drank milk and walked hundreds of kilometers on foot.

We prepared for the trip on a weekend, with two cars carrying six people. The road was not a straight line, nor were there many signs indicating the directions. Needless to say, there was also no GPS or Google Maps. We relied on the advice of those who had made that trip before. Parts of the road were non-existent, while other parts had perfectly tarred stretches. The interior of Gabon in those days seemed mostly empty of human habitation, except for a few scattered towns and villages.

I was in the car with the less adventurous members of this expedition. We tried to keep an eye on each other in the two cars to know immediately if something went wrong. And something did go wrong. The leading vehicle of our two-car convoy suddenly disappeared. One second, it was there, maybe 500 meters ahead of us, and the next second, it was gone. No human being or vehicle was in sight. We stopped our car roughly near the point where we had last seen the disappeared car. Two of us got out of the car while the person driving remained in his seat. We looked all around the bush, and we couldn't see anything. The road was built at a considerably higher level than the ground on either side. The bush on the side of the road was about one meter lower. Not finding anything on the right side of the road, we looked over the opposite side.

A little farther away, I saw a commotion in the bush. We crossed the road and walked towards the suspected area. We noticed one of our guys standing alone just below the road, without the car and the other two fellows. When we reached him, he told us what happened. While driving along at a considerable speed, for this was one of those smooth patches of the road, they suddenly saw a small goat running in the middle of the road. Their driver tried to avoid the goat, but the wheels skidded, and the car made a 180-degree spin. It continued in the opposite direction and fell into the ditch. He had stayed near the road so we could find him while the others were trying to see how to bring the car back on the road again.

Together, we reached the car. It was indeed about a meter deep in the ditch. It looked hopeless, and there was no way anyone could drive it out. Our cars were city sedans without the towing hooks and chains. We took turns to try to reverse the car out, and while the wheels kept spinning, the car wouldn't move. We had no idea what to do. Leaving the car in the middle of the jungle did not sound like an acceptable option as it belonged to our employers. We were not supposed to go on adventurous tours on those vehicles. It would have been very difficult to explain the whole thing to the office.

While we were desperately contemplating our next move, we heard a humming sound coming from one corner, followed by some footsteps. Some people were coming towards us through the jungle. One by one, they appeared in sight, a group of about fifteen men. They were mostly topless and carrying machetes or shovels. This did not look reassuring. Anything could happen. And the most unexpected thing actually did.

The men approached us and greeted us in French. They offered their help to move the car out of the bush. Of course, we said yes, but the question was, how would they do that? They kept humming a song or a chant and positioned themselves all around the car. The singing got louder and more passionate as they caught hold of the chassis of the vehicle. Those fifteen or so individuals raised the car with their bare hands and stepped over to the roadside. They changed the direction of the car to place its front wheels on the road and then pushed together to bring the entire vehicle on the road.

This entire exercise was like a miracle happening before our eyes. The car was back on the road and looked fine, other than a few scratches and dents. We thanked them profusely and offered some tips in cash that they flatly refused to accept. They picked up their chant and walked back into the forest while waving goodbye. Who were these people? We would never know.

After this trip, we asked several of our Gabonese friends about the incident. They were as surprised as we had been.

Nobody seemed to have the slightest clue about these people. They looked like people who would work in the agricultural or timber industry. All I can say is that they were a well-organized team. They enjoyed their chorus song that would go up and down in volume and intensity, depending upon what they were doing.

After the loss and eventual recovery of one of our vehicles by mysterious chanting men, we continued our journey toward Lambarene. As we approached the town, we realized that we were about an hour behind schedule.

Lambarene, Gabon

The thick vegetation and the overwhelming presence of the Ogooué River around the town added to the usual humidity-laden air that is typical of the region. The hospital complex was easy to locate, and our host waited right by the entrance. It seemed that the news of our entry into town reached her through another person. She welcomed us and commended us for making the journey.

She told us that the hospital where Dr. Schweitzer lived and worked until his death in 1965 had been preserved and transformed into a museum. A modern hospital was built much later, right next to the historical site, by the Albert Schweitzer Foundation. This hospital provides modern medical care to the zone. In fact, patients from various parts of Gabon come for treatments at this hospital due to the wide range of medical and surgical facilities available.

She told us that when Dr. Schweitzer first arrived in Lambarene in 1912, he had built his first and very rudimentary facility (ASH 1) on the river bank. This small clinic was in ruins when he came back to Lambarene after the end of World War I. Upon his return in 1924, he rebuilt this clinic (ASH 2) with the help of the locals and some of his companions from Europe. Very soon, this new facility proved insufficient because of the overwhelming number of patients coming from the surrounding areas.

The impact of the war was felt even in this remote region, where a lack of food and medical supplies created new outbursts of endemic diseases. Dr. Schweitzer then decided to build a new hospital, this time on the other side of the river (ASH 3). This new facility, which was completed in 1927, was designed like an African village. It had areas for outpatients, consultations, resident patients, a dining space, a surgery section, and spaces for the family members accompanying the patients. A main concern for Dr. Schweitzer had been the treatment of leprosy that was rampant in the region. He gradually treated and cured a large number of patients, but due to the social stigma attached to the disease, it was not easy for those who fully recovered to return to their communities. So, the hospital provided them with accommodation in an adjacent area, which became a large village over the years. Dr. Schweitzer called it "Village Lumière," or the village of light.

She showed us the old hospital, including the living quarters of Dr. Schweitzer. They were small and modest rooms with his working desk, books, pens, papers, and his famous piano that had been brought in upstream on the Ogooué River with the help of the captain of a ship. The various parts of the old hospital had been very well preserved and maintained as historical relics. She explained that improvements were made constantly over the facilities in the hospital with the help that continued to grow and arrive from different parts of the world after Dr. Schweitzer received the Nobel Prize for Peace. His reputation and the international recognition of his work generated a lot of interest, visits, and donations.

We learned from her, and I had heard some of it from my Gabonese friends, that Dr. Schweitzer, despite all his achievements, remained a controversial figure on many accounts. Firstly, he was accused by many of the hospital staff and others of being paternalistic and despotic. He allowed for practices on the hospital premises that would not have been acceptable in a modern hospital facility elsewhere, such as the presence of various animals around the hospital. Sanitation and hygiene on the premises was not really a big concern for him.

Secondly, he set up clear segregation between the Europeans and the Africans present on the premises, either as patients or as staff members. Thirdly, he believed in his own form of Christianity, which he developed as a theologian and scholar. He addressed the congregation at the hospital church every Sunday and preached his own beliefs.

As she was showing us around the large complex, we were completely overwhelmed by the speed at which she walked. We had to almost run to keep pace with her. I had been suspicious earlier when she told me that she walked over 230 kilometers from Lambarene and back. But watching her walk at the hospital, it seemed like she possessed tremendous energy, stamina and speed.

When the visit ended, she offered us water and milk to drink. We politely declined the milk, and she disappeared immediately. Our next task was to find a place where we could spend the night. But before that, we needed to have a very late lunch or an early dinner. We tried to find a restaurant, but nothing was open at that hour. Good thing we carried snacks and some cans of corned beef, which we ate.

Later, we found a makeshift motel where we managed to spend the night, and the next morning, we hit the road to return to Libreville. It was a memorable trip. After all these years, I remember it like it was yesterday. And the mysteries encountered remain, until today, unsolved.

4.2 A Memorable Cricket Match

The year was 1983. I was living in Gabon. Some of my friends who had played cricket when they were kids came up with the idea of playing cricket in Gabon. This sounded at first like a pipe dream. Nobody had ever played cricket in Gabon, as far as we could imagine. These friends of mine were a mixed bag, made up of guys from the Indian subcontinent, Australia, Jamaica and, of course, the UK. The first question was where could we play. Some of us had large gardens, but certainly not large enough to play a real game of cricket. I had a friend who managed one of the biggest hotels in town. The hotel had large green lawns that were not used for any particular activity. My friend was a Swiss citizen. I spoke with him about the possibility of letting us play cricket on his hotel lawns. He was intrigued by the idea. But he had no idea how cricket was played. He had an Irish wife. She knew a bit about cricket and told him that it would be a good thing for the hotel, as it would bring traffic of expats and may generate food and beverage business for the hotel.

Once the space was secured for playing, there was the question of preparing the pitch. For those readers who are not familiar with cricket, the pitch is a rectangular strip that is prepared in the center of the ground where the real game takes place. Some of the cricket enthusiasts in our group worked in construction and public works. With the approval of the hotel manager, we brought in a road roller to flatten the ground and produce the rectangular space that was not exactly what a professional pitch is supposed to be, but it was close enough for us to begin our game. We had already imported a full kit of cricket balls, gloves, bats, pads, wickets etc. In those days, wearing helmets while playing cricket was not the norm.

We began with very casual Sunday cricket. It was good fun. We discovered that there were some good cricket players among us. I was a terrible batsman. But I could deliver left-arm spin balls that were quite deceptive for the batsmen—a few weeks passed by like this. The hotel guests and other visitors also began to enjoy our weekly sport. One Sunday, our British friends who played with us told us that the British Embassy is very pleased with the advent of cricket in Gabon. They would like to hold a match between a British team and a rest-of-world eleven. Everyone thought that it was a great idea. So far, we have played in a very informal manner. The teams were decided on the spot. We never had enough players to have teams of eleven players each. We had no umpires, either. The idea of a real match meant that we had to do quite a bit of organization. We agreed to hold the match in three weeks. The British players very quickly distanced themselves from the rest of us to prepare their team. We heard that they were going to import some players from the town of Port Gentil, where the British petroleum company was based.

It Began In Africa

The "rest-of-the-world eleven", meanwhile, could not reach the number of eleven players. With all our effort, we were able to convince just seven players to play in the upcoming match. This was not looking good. Luckily, some Americans volunteered to play on our side. They were young and physically fit guys. The only inconvenience was that they had never played cricket. But they were willing to learn on a fast-track basis. So, we started some on-the-ground training and coaching for these gentlemen who were really very excited to learn this game and play on our side. We found out during the training sessions that they could hit the ball really hard as batsmen. But when they would run to score, they would drop the bat (not allowed in cricket, but a standard practice in baseball). They turned out to be really good fielders. They could run and grab the ball really well and could aim the wickets directly. On the other hand, bowling for them was not seen as feasible at all as they were used to baseball-style pitching, which is considered a 'no ball' in cricket. This was more than what we would have expected. Therefore, four Americans were hired to join our team, which would face the British team at the match. Both sides carried on with preparations. We heard that the British ambassador was taking a lot of interest in the match and had agreed to be present on the ground to watch the game.

Finally, the day of the match arrived. All players of our team, with their families and friends, arrived at the hotel cricket ground. Upon our arrival, we noticed that the British team and their supporters had already taken a position. They had put the British Union Jack flags on their side and set up a special seating arrangement with a VIP area where the ambassador was supposed to sit. We noticed that they had brought iceboxes full of Champagne and other beverages. The mood on the British side was very upbeat. As we were settling down, we saw the arrival of a trophy that the ambassador had ordered to be given to the winning team. Even before the match began, the supporters of the British team started chanting and rooting for their side. This whole buildup seemed quite overwhelming to the "rest-of-the-world" side, which had no flags, ambassador, champagne, or trophies. I was already imagining their impending victory in the context of the history of British involvement in Gabon.

The British had had some contacts in the nineteenth century with the territory that is called Gabon today. They had established a trading post in Gabon when France had not officially declared Gabon as a colony, though they mostly controlled the territory. The British trading activity gradually winded down and ended. One of the trading houses from that period, however, continued to exist well into colonial times—at least in name—and the more remarkable sign of British presence in the region is a neighborhood in Libreville called 'Quartier London.' In the more recent past, the Shell Oil Company had been involved in offshore petroleum extraction in Gabon. During my stay in Gabon (during the early 80s), I witnessed a certain return of the Brits to Gabon. A British embassy was opened in Libreville. Barclays Bank established an office, and British Caledonian Airlines started a direct flight between London and Libreville. This match would have provided a new life to the British presence in this land.

The match began with a toss of a coin to decide which team would bat first. We had agreed to play on the basis of 25 fixed overs for each team. The British team won the toss and decided to bat. Their followers chanted at a higher pitch. They were celebrating the winning of the toss as if they had already won the match. The Brits' team sent out two opening batsmen to start their innings. We deployed our fast bowlers to contain them. The two batsmen began spectacularly. During the first over (there were six balls in one over), they scored seven runs. The enthusiasm among the supporters of the British team was rising with every ball bowled. Their batsmen played solid strokes and kept a high run rate. Our bowlers managed to get wickets at a steady pace, but the run rate with the British remained high. Whenever a wicket fell, each incoming batsman began with new vigor and scored consistently. Under the strong encouragement and applause

It Began In Africa

from their supporters, the British team reached a score of 126 runs with nine players out. This was a strong performance. The jubilant chants of their supporters were beyond control now. There was a short break for the players to get refreshed. Our opening batsmen put on protective gear and walked into the field while the British team organized their fielding positions and designated the bowlers.

The rest-of-the-world team began their inning in earnest. We were aware of our lack of depth in the batting department. It was evident during the first few overs that our batsmen were on the defensive. They were trying not to lose wickets, but the run rate was suffering due to this strategy. At the end of the tenth over, we had lost two wickets, but we had scored just 42 runs. Our run rate at 4.2 runs per over was considerably lower than our adversaries, who had kept a rate of 6 runs per over. Things were not looking good. Our team captain, who was an accountant from India, decided to change the strategy and asked the batsmen to go aggressive. They followed the directive and started to hit hard on every ball. They were caught out very quickly. But the incoming batsmen continued the same approach. This went on till we lost six wickets. Now, the batsmen left were... the Americans. There were only five overs left, and the score was only 88. It meant that we needed 39 runs in five remaining overs. The required run rate per over was 7.8. It was an uphill task for any team at this stage in the game, as our strong batsmen were out. What we had left with was an untested bunch of Americans. Our American batsmen went to bat. We begged them not to drop their bats when running between the wickets. The British laughed at this sight. They seemed totally certain of their victory.

Our Americans did not show any stress whatsoever. They hit the ball hard, scoring fours and even a couple of sixers. They apparently thought that regular strokes and running between the wickets to score without dropping the bats were too much to handle. So, they decided to stay on the crease and hit fours and sixes instead. The run rate climbed up; the British supporters kept booing our batsmen for their unorthodox batting style, for they would walk up half the pitch to hit the ball. The excitement was getting intense. At the end of the 24th over, the score had reached 118. The victory suddenly seemed within our reach. But our team still needed to score nine runs in the last over. We still had two wickets in hand. The suspense continued as our batsman was bowled out on the first ball of the last over. The next batsman, another American, did not show that they were under any pressure at all. He hit his first ball to the boundary without touching the ground. This was a sixer. Suddenly, there was a complete silence in the British camp. All chanting, booing and clapping had died down.

There were four more balls to go, and we needed to score three runs. The next couple of balls were so tightly bowled that the batsman could not do much. On the fifth ball of the over, he hit the ball with all his force, and the ball crossed the boundary again. Four more runs! We had won the match. What followed at the end of the game was chaos. The ambassador of Great Britain stood up, handed over the trophy quite unceremoniously to the captain of the rest-of-the-world team and left the ground without saying a word. There was no ceremony at all. The fans of the British team who were ready to open the champagne bottles kept very quiet. Our side of supporters were very small in numbers. There were other guests of the hotel who had also gathered to watch the game. Many of them had no clue how this game was played, but they applauded the winning team anyway.

One would think that this was the end of the story. The British lost and felt bad. We won but stayed very low-key. Everybody went home. No. Things went in a different direction. While watching the game, the British supporters had managed to consume an impressive quantity of intoxicating beverages. They felt disappointed and angry. After the initial shock of the loss, they returned to action. The cricket ground was next to the hotel swimming pool. Some of the supporters formed a group and picked up the captain of their team on their shoulders. When

It Began In Africa

I saw this, I thought they were trying to put on a brave face and honor their team in spite of the loss. But they had other plans. They carried the captain to the swimming pool and dropped him into the water with a giant splash. They did not stop at this. They went back and picked up other players, one by one, and started to throw them into the pool. The players and their friends did not appreciate this. They also ganged up and began throwing those who had dropped them in the pool. Soon, it was complete mayhem. The Brits were going crazy, throwing each other into the pool. Our team and supporters tried to stay away from this madness. We could see the hotel guests who were around the pool were totally in shock.

The hotel staff came to stop this activity, which had turned the pool area into a battlefield. But they could not stop the frenzy. A little later, the hotel manager arrived on the scene with his wife. They were angry. They shouted and screamed at the hooligans who had gone totally out of control. They were trying to throw pretty much anybody they could lay their hands on into the pool. The manager called for more security guards, and the situation was under some control. He then summarily announced the end of all cricket on the hotel grounds. Thus, cricket in Gabon came to an abrupt end within a few months after its emergence. We tried our best to convince the hotel manager to give us a second chance. Even the British ambassador personally apologized to the hotel management for the rowdy behavior of the British fans. But the damage was done. No more sports activities were allowed on the hotel lawns. I heard later that some people from the Indian subcontinent had found a space near the port area to play some cricket on a cemented floor. They used tennis balls to play. But we could not go back to the short-run glory days of cricket in Gabon.

CHAPTER 5

THE WINNER TAKES IT ALL

A Gambler's Tale – 1981

The year is still 1981. I was living in Gabon as a young expatriate banker. Libreville was a relatively small town with a large population of foreigners. The oil-based economy of Gabon had attracted a lot of French, American, and other international corporations to set up activities there. There were a lot of restaurants, bars, nightclubs, and casinos catering to the expats in town. There were three casinos in the city, but Gabonese citizens were not permitted to gamble there. The entry to the casinos was exclusively reserved for foreign citizens. It was a routine for the expats, especially during the weekends, to go to a casino after having dinner at a restaurant. Even bankers were seen regularly playing at the casinos. This is not the case anymore due to the more elaborate codes of conduct and ethics established by financial institutions later on. But this is how things were in the year 1981.

I would also visit casinos with my colleagues and friends from time to time. We would usually meet other friends and fellow bankers and play a few turns at the blackjack table or the roulette. None of us ever engaged in any serious gambling activity. It was more of a social outing. Having said that, we would notice several very experienced and seriously engaged gamblers in the casino. They came from different backgrounds and age groups and took their games very seriously. They were treated by the casino managers as their valued clients and were offered preferential treatment as compared to what we received as amateurs and casual visitors. There were separate tables with much higher stakes for those serious gamblers, even separate rooms with baccarat tables.

My friends and I would generally not last long in the casino. But sometimes, I would start watching a certain gambler play and stay longer. I read a novel by Fyodor Dostoevsky titled *The Gambler*, which tells the story of a compulsive gambler. This book inspired me to observe and study this type of people. I found it fascinating how gamblers could move into a special zone and completely forget their real lives.

I would often watch older Lebanese traders, sophisticated European executives, Senegalese goldsmiths, and occasional Chinese players reach that special zone. The intensity of their concentration in the game would transform their facial features. Their eyes would be glued to the hands of the croupiers shuffling the cards or spinning the roulette wheel, where the ball slowed down its rotation and finally fell into a numbered slot. Their expressions, depending on whether that particular turn was in their favor or against their bets, would range from shiny eyes and bright smiles, murmuring words in their native tongues, to utter shock, disbelief, horror and resignation. Some would praise their respective gods when winning. Others would curse and accuse the casino of cheating when they were losing.

During one such visit to the casino with friends, I noticed a rather young Korean fellow in a red shirt playing on a roulette table. He appeared to be intensely immersed in the game. He would move up and down the table to cover the numbers from 0 to 36 while stacking up his favorite numbers with much larger bets. As he reached out to place his chips, his shirt would get untucked from his trousers. Once the croupier announced,

"Rien ne va plus!" (No more bets), he would stand back and tuck his shirt while watching where the ball would fall.

I approached the table where this young man was playing to watch his game because he somehow stood out. He was relatively much younger than other players, but more importantly, his energy and concentration were fascinating. When I looked at him a little more closely, he seemed familiar. I tried to recall where I had seen him, but I could not recognize him beyond that vague feeling of familiarity. There were many Koreans in Libreville. They were all connected to a building complex that was built and owned by a South Korean corporation, whose main business was to import and sell Korean cars. In the building were also bars, a supermarket, restaurants, shops, and apartments. I would not call it a mall because the mall concept had not yet become popular. It was a high-rise building wherein shops and restaurants were spread on several floors. The Korean corporation and several other businesses in that complex were customers in the bank, and I used to see them as clients from time to time.

Kim placing his bets (my drawing)

It Began In Africa

They were an interesting lot when it came to communication. They had some basic English knowledge when they arrived in the country, and they would pick up some French to carry on their business. But very often, they would mix English and French without much concern about whether they were understood or not. There is a line that I shall always remember from one of my Korean customers. Talking about his language expertise, he declared, "I speak French, but I don't understand it."

I kept seeing the young Korean gambler every time I visited that casino. He was becoming a permanent fixture of that casino. Eventually, I found out who he was. He worked in the Korean car company's garage as an auto mechanic. I had probably seen him in that garage during a visit to check the inventory of imported cars that served as collateral for the credit facilities provided by the bank.

What was truly fascinating for me to watch was how this meek young man had transformed. He seemed to know everyone in the casino, and everyone knew him. He had been on a prolonged winning streak that seemed unchallenged. His betting amounts and winnings kept growing. The casino management allowed him to cross the upper limits of his bets. When he arrived at the casino, the regular customers and the entire staff of the casino, such as the croupiers, floor managers, bartenders, and servers, would greet him, and he would respond like a star, waving his hand and smiling with pride and satisfaction. He would be offered champagne by the casino as he began to gamble on the roulette table. His chips would be brought to him without any cash produced on the table. He had a running account with the casino by now. Every time he would make a big win, he would order drinks for everybody on the table. He would tip the casino staff generously. Everybody seemed to love him. Several well-dressed ladies would hover around him at all times. But he kept his eyes, and his mind concentrated on the game.

His looks also changed. He grew his hair much longer. He now wore silk shirts and often had a colorful sports jacket on.

He sometimes arrived with dark sunglasses covering his eyes. He had become famous, a celebrity of a kind. His name was Kim. People at cocktail parties and diplomatic receptions would talk about him. He had become a subject with which people would start. "Have you heard the latest about Kim, the gambler? He just bought a red Corvette." People would speculate how much money he had. They would wonder if he had a special gift to guess the right numbers to bet upon.

There were rumors that he had aligned with a Malian "marabout," a Muslim faith healer and fortune teller in Africa. Malian marabouts were all the rage in Gabon at that time. Even the president of the country had a Malian marabout of his own who would provide him with valuable inputs and leads about his actions and decisions. This presidential marabout became immensely rich, providing spiritual advice to the dignitaries of Gabon. He ran a transportation business in Mali with hundreds of trucks and buses.

Other than the Malian marabouts, there were the Beninese voodoo masters and the visiting Indian Swamis. The visiting Swamis would travel to several countries in Africa. They would get appointments with top government officials, ministers, and ambassadors. They were mostly fortune tellers with many tricks up their sleeves. They knew how to impress those dignitaries and, in return, get paid handsomely.

Although our Mr. Kim had become the talk of the town, nobody seemed to know him. People wanted to know: Where did he live? How did he come to Gabon? Where did he work, if he did work at all? Few knew even the little I knew. Hardly anyone had seen him anywhere else except at the casino. Nonetheless, his winning streak continued unabated. People began to notice that he wore diamond rings and gold bracelets. His tips to the casino staff became more and more generous. He was seen in casinos almost every night. He gambled until very late in the night and regularly kept winning large sums of money. I saw him a few more times in his full glory. It was a sight to behold every time. He hardly spoke any French. His English was minimal, but it did not matter. He was a character, larger than life. When he was in the casino, people treated him as if he were a legendary figure. They were happy to see him and honored to serve him.

But within a few months, his glorious winning spell began to falter. I heard from a friend that Kim had not been seen for a while in the casino. Kim favored one of the three casinos in Libreville, which was situated in a hotel called "Le Dialogue," but as his successes grew, he began to visit the other two casinos, too. So, if one did not see him on one particular night in his favorite casino, people thought that he must be gambling in one of the other two casinos. A couple of weeks after hearing about Kim's absence, I happened to be in his favorite casino, and he was not there. I asked one of the staff about Kim. She replied in a quiet tone that he may not be feeling well.

The garage that Kim worked for was managed by a much older Korean man who visited my bank from time to time for his banking transactions. A few days later, I saw him in the banking hall. Since I was really curious about Kim, I stopped the manager and asked about him. He knew very well who I was referring to, but he replied that there were many Kims in his company. Which one I was referring to? I hesitated to say "the famous gambler" to Kim's employer and just said that I was talking about the young auto mechanic. He told me that Kim had been down with malaria and had been absent from work for several weeks. Soon, it was found out that he owed money to a lot of people, so they were trying to find out what was going on with him, too. I told him that if he needed any help from the bank, do not hesitate to contact me. He thanked me and left.

The garage manager called me the same afternoon and asked for an appointment. We agreed to meet the next day. He came to my office with a large file, put it on my desk, and opened the folder. It was full of unpaid checks, invoices, utility bills, and restaurant bills, among other things. He explained that Kim had been spending money far beyond his means and had piled up a huge debt. He had not been working normally for months. He would come to work very late in the morning, always looking tired. Medical checks were done on him, but the doctors could not find anything wrong.

I did not know what to say. My legendary hero was falling apart before my eyes. He continued to tell me that beyond those unpaid bills, there was also a huge sum that he owed to someone who sold him a luxury car. The manager had still not mentioned a word about Kim's gambling life, so I was reluctant to bring it up. I could understand that in a traditional Asian working environment, this would be embarrassing to mention. But it was the elephant in the room, stamping around while we sat politely. Finally, I reluctantly brought it up by saying that Kim was very popular in the city casinos.

The face of the manager fell at the mention of the casino. He admitted that that was the worst part. Kim owed huge sums to the casino, bigger than his other debts. He began signing IOUs after losing money. He was particularly worried about Kim's safety because he heard that the casinos may be owned by a dangerous mafia. I controlled my smile at the mention of the mafia. Indeed, the people who owned the casinos were not straightforward business people. One of the casinos was owned by the family of a French politician from Corsica of dubious reputation named Charles Pasqua, who later became a minister of interior under President Jacques Chirac.

The story of Kim ended for me when his employer finally decided to send him back to Seoul after clearing up his unpaid bills and debts. The rumor was that the casino owners forced the Korean company to pay off his IOUs.

Charles Pasqua – A French minister

CHAPTER 6

A FLYING ADVENTURE

Elephants and Planes – 1982

I am not an adventurer by any stretch of the imagination or interpretation of the term. In fact, I have always lived a protected and comfortable life in safe and secure locations in Africa. I admire those Westerners who come to Africa with their backpacks, traveling boldly across the deserts, forests, rivers, and even war zones using the most basic means of transportation like motorbikes, trucks, bush taxis, etc. In my case, I have never tried to go on an adventure.

But things happen from time to time…

My boss asked me to make a trip to the coastal town of Port-Gentil, where the bank was constructing a building to house a branch office. I was tasked to review the progress of the project. The contractor for the project was a young French architect who lived in Libreville but used to travel frequently to Port-Gentil. I contacted him to coordinate my visit, and he promptly proposed that I travel with him on a plane that he would pilot himself rather than on a regular Air Gabon flight. I agreed without much discussion. I had not given much thought to the kind of aircraft we would take until the morning of the flight.

I arrived at the airport and went to the zone reserved for small private planes and trainer aircraft. When I arrived there, my contractor-pilot was busy on the tarmac with the plane. It

It Began In Africa

was a Cessna two-seater. It was smaller than a normal car. I was taken aback. There were a couple of ground personnel who were checking the plane to make sure that everything was in working order. We greeted each other, and I boarded the plane. My pilot took my bag and placed it behind our seats. Everything felt shaky, rickety and wobbly on the plane.

Then I realized that I was the copilot on this flight. This plane was used for training pilots, and the two people had access to the controls for training purposes. The Cessna two-seater is a single-engine plane. And the engine makes a lot of noise. When the pilot turned on the engine and the propeller started to spin, everything started to blur around us. The aircraft started to move from the tarmac to the runway.

In no time, we were in the air. The takeoff for a tiny plane is rather quick. The pilot kept talking on the plane radio with the air traffic control. It was actually a great feeling to fly like this. I could follow every move that the pilot was making. It was fascinating to observe how the little rickety machine behaved much more firmly and solidly in the air compared to when it was on the ground.

My pilot seemed very proud to show off his flying skills. He asked me if I would like to see a herd of elephants in the forest. I had heard of herds of elephants roaming around in the jungles of Gabon, but nobody seemed to have actually seen them. Primarily because the forest is so dense and impenetrable that casual visitors have no business in such a place. So, naturally, I said yes, I would like to see a herd of elephants. The pilot swiftly made the plane turn towards the east. Now, instead of flying over the ocean, we were above the lush green forest. He had a pair of binoculars that he used to look down on the forest below us, then he gradually reduced the flying altitude to have a much better view. He swayed the plane left and right to search for elephants. He seemed to be well-experienced in that task. He told me that this was the time of the year when elephants moved in large herds in that area. And we were not disappointed. He located a large group of dark creatures that turned into elephants as we got closer. It was a moment of pure joy and exhilaration. Such a grandiose display of wild nature! Our plane made a couple of circles over the herd.

This was when I noticed that it had started to rain. The sky looked clear, but the rain was coming sideways. And when I looked in the direction where the rain was coming from, I had to rethink what I said about the sky being clear. It was pitch dark on the other side. And this dark mass of rain clouds was heading towards us. The elephants probably knew in advance about the coming rainstorm, which was why they were moving away from it.

My pilot tried to raise the plane to a higher altitude, deploying all the force from the single engine that we had. We did move upward, but the sudden gush of wind and rain smacked our plane sideways. The sky had gone dark. All the control displays in front of me were going crazy. The plane shook, bumped up and down, and swayed left and right like an autumn leaf in the wind. The calm and rather comic disposition of the pilot was gradually beginning to change as he frantically turned the various knobs and controls on the dashboard. But he kept telling me to stay calm. The noise of the aircraft, the rain, the wind and the sound of my own heartbeat were not letting me follow what he was telling me. He was most probably saying that these storms are common in these areas and there was nothing to worry about, etc.

In this chaos, I noticed that the radio had gone silent. We had lost contact with the airport in Libreville. GPS was not yet invented. The only navigation tool for pilots was a compass on the plane and radio contact.

The plane kept moving in random directions without any focus, and this showed in the way the compass needle was turning erratically. The pilot told me that storms are either on the land or on the sea and that he was trying to move the plane to the west to reach the coast. Meanwhile, I was also worried about the fuel levels. We had been flying for a far longer time than the scheduled flight duration. It felt like the end to me. I said to myself that this was probably the time when your entire life ran through your mind like a movie. Then I realized that it would be a really short movie, considering that I was only twenty-three years old.

I remember that I was just sitting with my two hands resting over my face when I felt drops of water falling over my hands. The plane had started to leak. Rainwater inside the plane. I was absolutely horrified. But suddenly, something weird happened—the plane was sucked upwards at a crazy speed by some anti-gravitational force that I was unaware of. After that upward pull, the plane stabilized a bit and seemed to start going in one direction. My pilot had managed to drag the plane towards the sea.

I could see the ocean from a distance. Soon, we were flying over the waters of the Atlantic Ocean. There was much more light and visibility. There were still a lot of clouds, but the rain reduced to a drizzle. We were back to life! With some maneuvers on the radio dial, the pilot established communications with the Port Gentil airport traffic control. The traffic controllers seemed to be more excited by our survival than the two of us sitting on the plane. They were screaming, "*Bravo, Jeannot! Tu es le champion!*" (Good job, Jeannot! You are the champion!). Within the next fifteen minutes or so, we were landing at the little airport of Port-Gentil. I looked at the time and realized that we had flown for 105 minutes for a flight that would normally last forty minutes. Here is the flight path that I have recreated with the help of Google Maps:

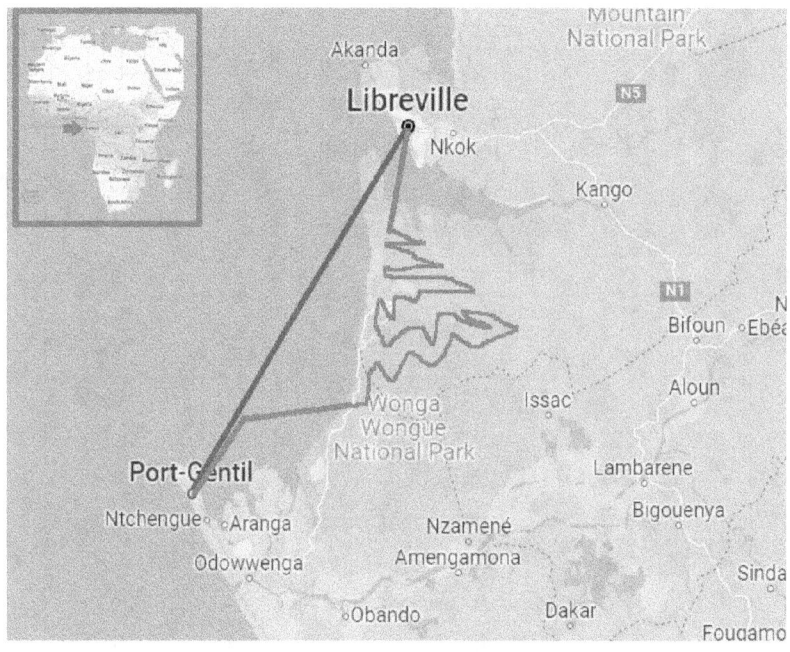

The blue line shows the normal flight path. The red line shows the actual path that the flight took.

The air traffic control staff, the airport security teams, and the pilot's friends had already taken a position on the tarmac before our plane made a complete stop. Some were holding bottles of champagne. It was a triumphant reception. My pilot kept telling everyone how calm his passenger was during the crisis. I was not calm at all, but I had somehow given him that impression. Over the years, I have realized that everybody thinks

I am a calm person. This is not the reality. It may look so, but inside, the wheels of worry and concern are often turning at full speed.

We ended up having a festive lunch at a French bistro, and the party continued.

CHAPTER 7

AN APARTHEID STORY

How to Become an Honorary White Person – 1986

The year was 1986. I was now based in Abidjan, Côte d'Ivoire, as I was transferred with a huge promotion in 1985 to head the bank there. I was asked by the head office in London to attend the annual general meeting of the African Development Bank (AfDB). AfDB is Africa's regional development finance institution. Its headquarters are located in Abidjan, Côte d'Ivoire, so it would have been very easy for me to attend a meeting there. However, the AfDB holds its meetings in different parts of the continent. This time, the meeting was scheduled in Harare, Zimbabwe.

Traveling within Africa was not easy in those days. The situation has improved since then, but it still remains complicated. In those days, traveling from Abidjan to Harare required multiple connections and long layovers with strong possibilities of delays, missed connections and lost baggage. Luckily, I was called for another meeting in London that was scheduled a couple of days before the annual general meetings of AfDB. This made my trip much easier because there were regular flights from London to Harare. Before going into my story, there is some important context to be aware of.

Zimbabwe was called Rhodesia until 1980. It was run by a white-minority regime on similar lines as South Africa under apartheid. The minority regime in Rhodesia emerged in 1965 in a unilateral act of independence from Britain. Before this, it was a self-governed British colony. The imposition of institutionalized racial discrimination immediately provoked resistance from the black majority population, and a civil war ensued that went on for about fifteen years. The United Nations and the Organization for African Unity imposed sanctions on Rhodesia similar to those imposed on South Africa.

The resistance forces were divided into two groups: The Zimbabwe African National Union (ZANU) led by Robert Mugabe and the Zimbabwe African People's Union (ZAPU) led by Joshua Nkomo. The old colonial masters (Britain) sponsored negotiations between the warring parties, and an agreement was reached to organize all-inclusive elections to restore majority rule in the country. However, there were many legal and constitutional hurdles to the process.

Though such elections were held, the white minority ruled by Ian Smith still kept a strong position. Bishop Abel Muzoreva, who became prime minister of this setup, could not achieve peace, and international efforts continued to search for a lasting solution. The British Commonwealth and the British government led these efforts to organize a conference between the three top leaders of the majority population (Robert Mugabe, Joshua Nkomo and Abel Muzoreva) in late 1979.

This conference resulted in the Lancaster Agreement that ended the civil war. It also reversed the unilateral declaration of independence that was made in 1965 by the minority regime of Ian Smith, and Rhodesia (now Zimbabwe) returned to British colonial rule. The international sanctions against the country were also lifted. This allowed Britain to supervise elections in the country. The elections held in early 1980 brought the party of Robert Mugabe (ZANU) to power as the country formally and finally gained independence from Britain.

Ian Smith (my drawing)   Robert Mugabe (my drawing)

Robert Mugabe, who had openly expressed support for Bishop Abel Muzoreva, was elected against the wishes of the British government. In those days, I was a regular reader of *The Economist* magazine. They used to give the impression that the Bishop was far ahead in popular support. All these speculations and expectations proved to be wrong. Mugabe assumed his office with great international support. The African states strongly welcomed the end of the white minority regime and the emergence of a modern African state.

One of the main issues that the new government faced was how the agricultural land was divided in the country. Most viable agricultural lands were owned by white farmers. This was clearly a very unfair state of affairs that needed a solution. The British government offered to financially sponsor a land reform under which the white farmers would be compensated for the land that they would be required to relinquish in favor of African farm workers who would then gain land ownership.

But Robert Mugabe refused to implement any such reform and declared that white farmers were citizens of Zimbabwe and their land ownership rights would be protected by his government. This situation would explode later. It was going to cause massive disruption and breakdown of the economy and the state of Zimbabwe under the leadership of Robert Mugabe. But that is another story.

Let's go back to my visit to attend the annual general meeting of the African Development Bank in Zimbabwe. At the time, neighboring South Africa was under the apartheid regime. When I booked my flights from London to Harare, I found out that while I would fly non-stop to Harare, there was no direct flight available out of Harare on the day I had planned to return. The only possibility was to take a flight from Harare to Johannesburg (South Africa) and then take a South African Airways flight back to London. Of course, my final destination was Abidjan, Côte d'Ivoire, but due to the sanctions imposed by the Organization for African Unity (OAU) against the South African regime, most African countries had no air links with South Africa except the immediate neighbors of South Africa, who were very closely connected despite the political divide. Therefore, I had to get back to London and then go to Abidjan.

My trip to Harare went great, and it was my first trip to Zimbabwe. It is a beautiful country with perfect weather. In 1986, the city of Harare (Salisbury, until recently) gave the impression of a cute little town in England during the summer, with red brick houses, flower gardens, and a safe, friendly atmosphere. Little did I know that all this would go through major turmoil and degradation within a few years.

The inauguration ceremony of the Annual General Meeting of the African Development Bank was presided over by Robert Mugabe himself, who made a brilliant speech that lasted over one and a half hours. He spoke about a new era for Africa and how the days of the apartheid regime in South Africa were numbered. How he would bring the whole continent together, win all the freedom fights, and bring a new era of success and prosperity for all Africans. Everybody was deeply impressed and generally fascinated by his charisma and oratory. Few people outside Zimbabwe knew that behind this magnificent façade lurked a cynical and vicious individual who had, just two years after taking over the reins of the country, perpetrated a murderous attack on the tribal lands (Matabeleland) of one of his political allies, Joshua Nkomo.

The annual general meetings of the multilateral development banks such as the World Bank, Asian Development Bank, African Development Bank, or Inter-American Development Bank are not just the solemn gatherings of their member countries but also serve as a large forum and meeting point for many people from the world of economics and finance around the world. There are commercial and investment bankers, consultants, and experts who work with the development banks, IT companies, inspiring startups looking for funding, venture capitalists looking for deals, and hordes of journalists and media people who not only cover the event but find many hard to reach personalities for media talks and interviews. The main event is often overshadowed by a series of side events, seminars, receptions, workshops, lunches, and dinners.

I experienced all these events in accordance with the guidelines of my employer and also stole some time to visit the town and its surroundings. It was a short trip of five days. It came to an end quickly, and I embarked upon my return journey that was going to take me for a few hours to Johannesburg, South Africa.

It was my first time visiting South Africa. It was not even a visit but just a layover at the airport. I was not sure what to expect. It was just a two-hour flight on a small South African Airways plane. The plane, though small, looked in good repair. The crew was all white, as I had expected. Their uniforms were crisp and reminded me of the 1960s. The service was minimal but efficient.

When the plane landed at Johannesburg airport, the first thing that struck me was the large number of armed soldiers in combat gear waiting on the tarmac. It was a scary sight; it seemed as if they were going to arrest all the passengers as we deplaned. When I stepped out of the aircraft on the gangway, I could see that there were two of those soldiers positioned right on top of the gangway. It was intimidating. I walked down to the bus that took the passengers to the transit lounge. My passport and ticket were checked a few times by people in different uniforms. I could not help noticing that all the soldiers and airport staff were white.

Since I was in the business section of the lounge, food and drinks were available and neatly placed on a spread. I had some tea and a snack. A lady in a South African Airways uniform approached to inform me that my connecting flight to London would be delayed further by three hours. Therefore, I had more than six hours to spend waiting in the lounge. However, the airline had a complimentary service that would allow me to go on a city trip on a bus and have lunch in town before coming back to the airport. This sounded like a great idea, but I realized that I did not have a visa for South Africa. Not only that, I did not want to have a South African immigration stamp on my passport, for this could put me in trouble in several countries in Africa, not to mention my own home country.

I expressed my apprehensions to the airline lady. She outright dismissed my worries. She told me that I did not need a visa. Not only that, but they would also not stamp my passport. They would just keep my passport and issue me an entry-exit card that I would be required to keep on myself during the excursion and present to the staff upon my return to the airport to recover my passport. This sounded great, so I agreed to go on the trip. I thought that it was a unique opportunity to look at this country, which was out of bounds for me under normal circumstances.

The airline lady took me to the immigration counters. The immigration officers were also dressed in combat gear, just like the soldiers that I had seen on the tarmac upon landing. They spoke in Afrikaans with the airline lady. After looking at me and my passport a few times, he completed the entry-exit card and put a couple of stamps on it. He handed the card to me and kept my passport. It looked like a regular government document except for one thing. The second stamp that he had affixed on the card was just out of this world! It said in bold letters: "HONOURARY WHITE."

While walking away from the immigration counters with the lady, I asked her about this strange stamp. She smiled and informed me that international passengers could be granted the status of honorary whites for a short period. They can visit those areas in the city that are designated as international. Nobody had ever told me about this. I went along and boarded the bus. There were several other passengers on the bus who were, like me, coming from the event in Harare, Zimbabwe. Most of them were truly white and, unlike me, did not require a special stamp to go on this ride.

The trip was very well put together. We went through the streets of the downtown of Johannesburg. At that time, it was the business center of the country. We saw neatly manicured green areas, trees, flowers, and impressive high-rise buildings that housed head offices of banks, insurance companies, and large corporations. The sidewalks seemed mostly empty of people, thanks to a very strict system of reserved access.

After the tour of the designated zones of the city, we made a stop at a nice restaurant. It was a traditional European restaurant that served excellent food, including the famous South African beef and seafood. The restaurant staff was all white. So far, we have hardly seen a nonwhite person. Everyone was in good spirits after such a great lunch. Soon, it was time to get back to our bus and return to the airport. On our way back, I caught a glimpse of a walled zone that was secured with barbed wires. It was only visible for a few seconds, but I noticed that the walled zone was over a hill. Later on, I found out that it was a black township of Johannesburg that was suitably hidden from the eyes of international travelers.

As the bus reached the airport terminal and the passengers entered the building, I needed to use the restroom, so I followed the signs to get there quickly. As I was entering the restroom, a uniformed employee stepped in front of me and told me in no clearer terms that I was not allowed to use that washroom. I must go to the washroom located on the other side of the building, which is allocated for "coloreds." I hesitated at this point. I considered the option to brandish my card, which granted me the status of honorary white. But I decided to pass. I just said, "Fine," and thought, "When in Rome…" I rushed towards the general direction of the other restrooms. And I found one rather fast.

But before I could enter, a similarly dressed employee, as the last time, intercepted me and told me that this restroom was for "blacks" only. Please go to the appropriate restroom for your race. This was getting annoying by now. I asked this person to kindly show me the restroom for the colored people. He asked me if I was not white. I assured him that although I had a piece of paper that granted me the status of honorary whiteness, I would rather not use it here. My need to reach the restroom was getting more pressing with every passing second. Luckily, the appropriate restroom was not too far away, and I finally managed to relieve myself—so much for being an honorary white.

The plane that I took to fly back to London was much bigger and more comfortable than the one I had taken from Harare to Johannesburg. The service was excellent. The food and drinks were of very high quality. It was supposed to be a non-stop flight, so I was completely taken by surprise when the pilot announced that they would make a technical stop at the Abidjan airport. What? That was my final destination. "Could I just disembark there?" I asked a crew member. I was told that that would not be possible. The plane landed and parked in the dark at a far corner of the airport. There was refueling and unloading of cargo before taking off again for London.

I was deeply disappointed to arrive at my town like this without being allowed to disembark. Why did this happen? Apparently, the sanctions imposed by the Organization for African Unity (OAU) were not strictly followed by some countries such as the

Côte d'Ivoire. There were secret arrangements to allow landing for refueling and also to transport South African goods to the country that were highly in demand and were sold in certain exclusive stores.

CHAPTER 8

THE HIDDEN SIDE OF AFRICA: SECRET SOCIETIES, VOODOO, MAGIC

Watching Voodoo Spells Unfold Firsthand – 1993

This story is from Benin, and the timeframe is the early '90s. I was running a newly established bank in Benin that was a part of a regional banking group. I had a small team of executives who were well-experienced in their respective areas and came from other well-established banks. One of these executives was Abdou. He was Senegalese and had been trained by Citibank in West Africa. He was responsible for the credit and marketing division of the bank. It was a key position, and I relied heavily on him for both the quality of credits that the bank approved and the business development in general. He was a single man in his late thirties, very dedicated to his profession and work ethic.

The story starts when Abdou began to arrive late for work. At first, it was about thirty minutes or so, but it got worse. Over time, his energy and work output began to falter. I asked for a chat with him to find out what was the matter. I had deliberately set up the time at 8:00 a.m. to see if he would show up on time.

He did not arrive at 8:00 a.m. but appeared in my office at 10:30 a.m. I let him in to talk. He looked visibly different. His usual sharp, energetic, and smiling demeanor was gone. He appeared tired and dull. He told me that he was very sorry to be late for the appointment. He was having some health issues that made it difficult for him to come to work on time. I asked him if he had referred to the bank's physician. He said he had undergone several tests, but they had not found anything.

I asked him to describe his symptoms to me. He spoke in some detail about how he felt a total lack of energy to get out of his bed in the morning. He felt a pressure or a heavy weight on his shoulders. It was as if some force was holding him down. This pressure grows into a burning sensation upon his shoulders as if they were on fire. He could not move during the morning. It was around midday that his condition got a little better, allowing him to get out of bed, shower, eat something, and show up at work. This had become his routine for the last eight weeks. The bank's doctor had given him some pills, but they did not make any difference. I asked Abdou to give his doctor permission to discuss the details of his health condition with me. He did so immediately, and I had a chat with the doctor the next morning. The doctor told me the same story. He confessed that he was unable to find any medical reason for his condition. The various tests had not shown anything unusual.

I asked for the doctor's advice on referring this case to a higher medical authority. He fully agreed that it was the right way to go. He wanted to contact a hospital in Paris, but I preferred a hospital in London that received international patients. I contacted them and forwarded Abdou's medical history. The senior physician who was assigned by the hospital to deal with the case asked me to send the patient to London for a detailed diagnosis. Abdou traveled to London and underwent a complete medical checkup and tests. The assigned doctor kept in touch with me to inform me about their findings. Abdou had been a chain smoker and had some health issues related to that. While in London, he did not experience the morning syndrome that used to incapacitate him in Benin.

The doctors concluded that Abdou was physically fine other than his smoking issues. His complaint about the morning syndrome was, according to the doctors, probably a psychological complication that would require long-term psychiatric therapy. He got back to Benin, looking significantly better. He was hoping that his condition would be cured. But his problem came back on his first morning in Benin. It was a bit milder than before, but as the days passed, the condition intensified, and he became almost bedridden. He would come to work at around 3:00 or 4:00 p.m. He would try to work until late hours to catch up, but it was obvious that he was unable to assume his role. It was a real setback for me, too, because his role had been critical in the bank.

A few months passed by in this fashion. One Monday morning, I arrived at my office at my usual time of 7:30 a.m., and I saw Abdou chatting with my secretary, full of that energy and enthusiasm that used to characterize him before his problem started. I greeted him and asked him what was going on. He spoke with a big smile on his face: "Can I see you in your office?" I said yes, and we walked in. I noticed that he was carrying a sturdy plastic bag in red and white that was common in African markets.

Red and white plastic bag

This is what he told me. "I was afflicted with my condition so badly that during the weekends, I could barely manage to get out of my bed to reach the living room and lie on the couch. I was lying on my couch on Sunday at noon when a couple of my friends barged into my living room. They were accompanied by a very tall and turbaned man. This mysterious man had a younger and smaller version of himself right behind him. My body felt so weak that I could not even sit up to welcome them. I just said hello in a feeble voice. They came near me and shook my hand. Then they introduced me to this mystery man.

"One of my friends said that he was sick and tired of my malady. Although I had always refused to be treated by a traditional healer or a Marabout (as they were called here), they had decided to make an intervention and subject me to this one séance, whether I liked it or not. As you know, sir, I am a practicing Muslim, and I do not believe in occult science. I have always rejected treatment by any Marabouts. But my condition was so pathetic that I could not resist this friendly intervention.

"The Marabout and his sidekick quickly sprang into action. They cleared a floor area in my living room and set up several bonfires using firewood, which generated strong aromatic smoke around us. They pulled me down on the floor and removed my T-shirt so that I had no clothing on my upper body. They began a loud incantation in native tongues that I don't follow. They slapped their hands first on the floor and then on my torso. The song grew even louder, and the smell of burning wood overpowered me. This was when they started to draw objects from my body and throw them into the fires to burn. I knew you would certainly ask me what those objects were. So I have brought their burnt remains for you to see for yourself. The objects were either metallic, mostly nuts, rivets, bolts, or screws, or there were living creatures. These living creatures were pulled out of my shoulders and arms. They came out alive and kicking before they were thrown into the fire to burn."

With these words, he opened the red and white plastic bag and showed me the burnt objects. There were nuts and bolts but also some burnt remains of unidentifiable animals. One looked a bit like a lobster. Another looked like a giant scorpion.

He completed his account of the séance with these words: "The act went on for a long time, maybe forty-five minutes or so. Finally, the Marabout announced that he had removed all the evil objects from my body. He informed me that I was healed from the voodoo magic spell that I had been under. He said that it was someone who was jealous of my professional success who cast this spell on me. He advised me not to offend people because you never know who can have recourse to occult forces here in Benin."

My colleague Abdou was healed after this intervention. He could not explain in any logical terms how this all happened. Nor can I come to terms with the magical events that he went through. I did not become a believer in magic. I consider this to be one of the several unexplained events in the world that would remain unexplained.

CHAPTER 9

WHEN THINGS GO WRONG

A Comedy of Confusions – 1994

This is a story from 1994. I lived in Cotonou, Benin. It was summer vacation, and one of my daughters was staying with me while the rest of the family was supposed to be arriving from Canada. Their flight was supposed to land in Lomé, Togo. Togo is a country neighboring Benin. Togo had a more developed airport than Benin, and more airlines connected it to the rest of the world. The road trip between Cotonou and Lomé takes about two to three hours, depending on the traffic and the time spent crossing the borders. The plan was that my daughter and I, with our driver, would go by road to pick up the family members arriving in Lomé. Since the flight was scheduled to arrive in the evening, I had booked hotel rooms for the whole family to spend the night in Lomé and drive back to Cotonou the next morning. Nothing was challenging or difficult in this plan.

But things happen…

Whatever happened in this story can primarily be blamed on the delay in the invention of mobile phones. If those handy devices had been invented and made commercially available, we would have been saved from all the confusion.

We were on our way to Lomé and were not far from the border of Benin and Togo when I heard a strange short sound that seemed to come from below the car. It was a Peugeot 605, a high-end French sedan model that was redesigned to give it a modern and luxurious look. Among the revolutionary features that this car included was the transmission of gasoline from the tank to the engine through a plastic pipe that ran right under the belly of the car. This was part of a series of measures that were introduced to reduce the weight of the car, boost the mileage, and allow for the luxury features that add to the weight of the car. This plastic pipe was the other reason for our comedy of confusion that started with the weird sound.

I immediately called for the attention of my driver. He was driving along without a care in the world and had not heard the sound. My motto has always been, "If you see something, say something!" In this case, it was "If you hear something..." My driver hit the brakes to slow down, but the car made some strange sounds and came to an abrupt stop on its own. The engine stopped by itself. The fuel gauge indicated that the tank was completely empty. All the gas in the car was gone. The transmission pipe had been damaged by a pebble on the road. It was made of plastic. What a great idea to introduce plastic to transmit gas to the engine! French automotive engineering never ceases to amaze us.

Peugeot 605 circa 1993
Image Credit: BetterParts.org https://www.betterparts.org/peugeot/other/peugeot-605.html

Our car had stopped on the road near the Benin-Togo border without a drop of gasoline in its tank. Now what? It was getting dark. The night was going to fall soon. We were in the middle of nowhere. But our driver told us that we were not very far from the border. He got some gasoline from a small vendor somewhere in the bush in order to bring the car up to the border area where there were gas stations and some help available. The problem was that the transmission pipe was broken, and the gas would last just a couple of minutes before it was sucked out. We moved slowly, adding gas from a jerrican. This process took us a long time to cover about 6 kilometers to the border area.

Who can forget the Citroën DS? A car so revolutionary in its design and engineering concepts that almost nobody ever wanted to buy it in North America.

"Marketed as **Citroën DS,** it was known for its aerodynamic, futuristic body design and unorthodox, quirky, and innovative technology, and it set new standards thanks to both being the first mass production car equipped with hydro-pneumatic suspension, as well as disc brakes. The 1967 series 3 also introduced directional headlights to a mass-produced car." (Source: Wikiwand: Citroën DS www.wikiwand.com/de/articles/Citroen_DS).

We managed to pass the border and stopped at a gas station on the Togo side. I knew someone who was a prominent figure in Togo and had a farmhouse in that area. He was also one of the founders of the bank for which I worked. He built a beautiful farmhouse with exotic trees and plants and had ostriches and deer roaming around in his fields. We parked the car at the gas station, where the mechanics confirmed what we had suspected all along. I requested my driver to go to the farmhouse of this friend of mine and borrow a car. He took a motorbike taxi ride to go to this person's home and borrowed a car so that we could

It Began In Africa

continue our journey to the airport in Lomé. My daughter and I waited in our immobilized car.

By the time my driver came back, driving a Mercedes sedan, it was already well past the flight arrival time. The gentleman that my driver had approached for a car was extremely nice to give us one of his best vehicles. It took us another forty-five minutes to reach the airport. When we arrived, the airport was almost empty. The flight had arrived and left. My driver spoke to some porters who were still around. They confirmed that my family had arrived and left in a big car. I went inside the airport and was able to walk into the arrivals area without any hindrance. There was not a soul around to stop me. During the pre-9/11 times, these small airports had very little full-time security and surveillance.

I reached the immigration counters and saw a bunch of disembarkation cards stacked on one of the counters. Those cards were required to be filled in for each arriving passenger. I very quickly found all the cards filled up by my family. They indeed landed in Lomé. However, the question was: where did they go? Who picked them up?

It was getting late, and my daughter was hungry. I decided to go to the hotel where we had booked rooms. There was a chance that my family had gone straight to the hotel and was waiting for me there. However, there was no sign of them at the hotel. I got my daughter some room service dinner and kept wondering what to do. Since my family knew that we would stay in this hotel, and since I was not waiting at the airport upon their arrival, the logical thing for them to do would have been to proceed to the designated hotel. But no.

Again, had I known of their future invention, I would have lamented our lack of cell phones.

At that point, I concluded that my family must have decided to go straight to Benin. In that case, they will be arriving at my home soon. That would have been fine because I could call the house, and we would have been able to clear up the confusion.

But things were not that simple. I had all the keys to the house. And this was a weekend. What could I do now?

I recalled that one of the sliding French windows in my living room did not lock. I had some furniture stacked against it inside the living room, but if someone knew the secret of that sliding door, one could easily make an entry. Those were the days when the chance of a burglary in my neighborhood was close to zero. In addition, I had a security guard at the entrance. This loophole in the home security would save me now and allow my family to enter the house. But how do I let them know about this? Again, no cell phones.

I considered calling one of my colleagues or friends for help. In the end, I decided to call my secretary, who lived not too far away. I explained to her the situation, and she agreed to go to my house and wait for my family to arrive. She went there, and she waited, but they did not arrive. After a while, she went back to her apartment and told me on the phone that she had instructed the security guard to come over to her apartment in case my family arrived so that she could go there and let them in. For security reasons, she did not want to reveal the secret entry option to the security guard. As her boss, I concluded that she had handled the situation well. But where was my family?

My daughter had fallen asleep, and I was also on the verge of dozing off, confused and perplexed, when the phone rang in the room. It was the reception of the hotel. The person informed me that my family had arrived. What? Arrived from where? How? All these questions will be answered when we all get together to go through the events of the day. Right away, I rushed downstairs to the lobby to pick them up with their luggage and set them up in the two rooms that we had booked.

As they started to tell the story, my daughter and I kept interrupting them to ask why they did not wait at the airport. Many such questions flew back and forth. Finally, we finally found out what happened. When they landed at the Lomé airport, went through the security checks, and collected their bags, they looked for me outside the airport building. Instead of finding me, they found another driver from the bank that I worked for. He had been sent to pick up someone else who decided to take a hotel shuttle. So, the driver was going to call it a day and go home when he saw my family desperately trying to find me. The bank cars had a distinct license plate, and one of my daughters recognized it. At the same time, the driver, who knew us, also recognized my family. After some discussion, the driver contacted his supervisor through a public phone at the airport, who allowed him to drive my family to Benin.

They took the road that would take them to the border, and within forty-five minutes when they were very close to that zone, the driver saw my abandoned car and my original driver hanging out at the gas station. The two drivers, who knew each other, spoke and told their respective stories. My original driver explained that after dropping my daughter and me at the hotel, he went to return the Mercedes to its owner and had come back to the car to see if there was a chance to repair it. Otherwise, he would go to sleep in a motel and see what to do the next morning.

It was then decided that instead of crossing the borders, the family should return to the hotel in Lomé. And that is what they did. This is how they had finally arrived at the hotel. Everything worked out in the end—except for my question about why they decided not to go to the hotel in the first place and hit the road to Benin instead. They replied that since I was not at the airport, they thought that there was no point in going to the hotel. Because I would not be waiting at the hotel instead of showing up at the airport to pick them up. I am still intrigued by this answer. Their logic is lost on me. I guess I will never get this one. I ordered more room service food, and we kept asking each other random questions about the series of events of the day until we fell asleep.

CHAPTER 10

AN UNFORGETTABLE GIFT

Crocodile Handy – 1994

This is the story of an unforgettable gift that I received in Benin in 1994. My family was away, and I was on my own. My workday routine was to go home during lunch break because the lunch breaks were a long affair in French-speaking Africa. People generally went home at noon for a relaxed lunch and a siesta before returning to work around 2:30 to 3:00 p.m. I did the same: I went home, had a swim in the pool, and got some lunch, followed by a short nap before heading back to work.

But on one particular day, things did not go as per my routine—far from that. When I reached my house, I was taken aback to see my entire household staff standing outside the house by the garage gate. My driver signaled the security guard to open the gate, but the guard did not move. He motioned instead to lower the car window. I had no idea what was going on. I lowered the window on my side and asked the guard why he could not open the gate to let the car in. He walked near the car with his head down. He said in a grave tone, "There is a crocodile in there!"

"A crocodile in there?"

I could not make any sense of what the guard had just said. I was aware that I was in West Africa and crocodiles existed in the zone, but we lived in the prime residential district of the city.

It Began In Africa

Nobody had ever witnessed a crocodile in town. He confirmed that, yes, there was definitely a crocodile inside. This was why everybody, including the cook, the maid, the gardener, and the security guard, was waiting outside. I was trying to run through my brain all possible reasons why a crocodile might appear in my house. But there wasn't a plausible scenario that could explain the presence of a crocodile inside my house.

Finally, I decided to ask him the obvious question, "Where did it come from?" Where does anything come from? I was getting philosophical. The fact was that the crocodile was very much there. The guard remained very matter-of-fact. He said, "Chief Adé delivered it. He said that it was a gift for you!"

He further explained that the Chief arrived an hour ago with his two helpers. They brought the crocodile out of their vehicle with a rope tied around it. They put the crocodile in a little basin in the garden where the garden hose is kept for watering the lawn and the plants. They tied the crocodile to the faucet with the rope. I wanted to know why everyone was out if the crocodile was restrained with a rope. This time, the cook explained. He said that the rope was very thin and flimsy. It could break easily if the crocodile wanted to attack someone or just walk around the garden.

I thought about the risk and decided that we could keep a safe distance, but everybody had to get back inside and decide about the next steps. The garage gate was opened. My car and the staff entered the house. I stepped out of the car, and we approached the basin in the garden with extreme caution. Lo and behold! The crocodile was right there.

It was a surreal sight. It was a medium-sized crocodile that could hardly fit in that basin. Surely enough, a rope was tied around its thick neck and clumsily attached to the water pipe. My staff was right. This did not look safe at all, especially if one looked at the open mouth of the crocodile. It was scary.

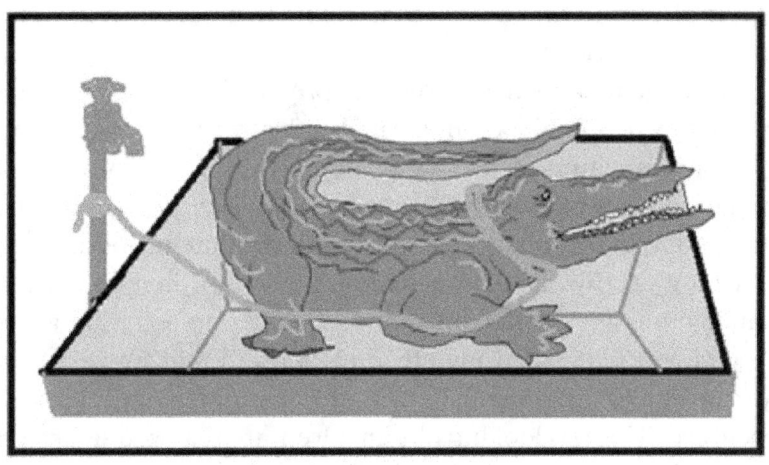

This crocodile was a gift. (my drawing)

We gathered outside the kitchen door so that we could quickly get inside if the crocodile made a move. They told me that the Chief had also brought a bucket full of fish to be fed to the crocodile. The guard had been throwing fish to the beast at regular intervals, apparently to appease it and to delay any acts of possible aggression. It was obvious that we could not run a normal household with a live crocodile around. The question was, what should we do about it? I asked the staff for ideas. The proposition from the maid was that we should kill the crocodile. I was not going to allow that. We would not be killing a wild animal in my house.

There must be something else. The security guard, whose name was Djima, spoke about a crocodile sanctuary that existed by the lake Ahémé. I had noticed the sanctuary, which was run by a group of followers of a traditional faith. They took care of crocodiles as a matter of religious duty. I had been offered to visit it, but I was not thrilled by the idea of walking between hundreds of crocodiles welcoming me with their open mouths. The sanctuary was about sixty kilometers away from my house. How would the logistics work? And would they accept our crocodile?

It Began In Africa

Djima offered to find out about it. He had a cousin or uncle who lived near the sanctuary.

This again happened during the pre-mobile phone era when contacting people was a complicated endeavor. But Djima showed great resourcefulness. He called the local mayor's office and spoke with someone who knew his cousin. That person fetched the cousin, and Djima spoke with him about the proposition to place a crocodile at the sanctuary. The cousin then visited the sanctuary to ask them if they would be open to receiving a live crocodile. I had called my office earlier and told my secretary to cancel all engagements in the afternoon as I was otherwise occupied. This was looking like an adventure that would take up the whole afternoon.

This process of transporting a crocodile seems beyond strange in hindsight. But at that moment, I was so deeply concerned about the presence of that animal at my home that I did not notice the strangeness of what we were trying to do. We had to wait for another hour. Djima went out to throw some more fish to the crocodile to keep it from making any menacing moves. Djima's cousin came back with positive news. The sanctuary was willing to receive the crocodile. They also gave some advice for transporting the animal. They suggested that we securely tie the jaws of the beast during the transportation and delivery.

Easier said than done, I thought. Who on earth could tie up the jaws of a crocodile? Djima volunteered to do it with the help of some of his colleagues in the security company.

He went off on his motorbike and came back with four security guards. It looked like they had already made their plan. They had a couple of jute bags and ropes in their hands. While my driver joined them in the action, the rest of us watched the scene from the kitchen window. They pounced on the crocodile and wrapped the jute bag around its head in a fraction of a second. Next, they used the ropes to tie his jaw that was under the jute wrap. They continued to wrap the ropes around its forelegs.

And this was not all. They had another jute bag that they tried to pull over its tail all the way to cover his legs. This was not easy because the tail was quite long if straightened. They somehow tied this second bag around the lower body of the crocodile, who wriggled vigorously at first but calmed down eventually. Then, they had to carry this bundle to the trunk of the car. The driver had positioned the car in such a way as to make the distance from the location of the crocodile to the car the shortest possible. They synchronized their act, and the six of them grabbed the bundle. They moved rather slowly towards the car because they did not want to drop their catch. When they reached the trunk of the car, they placed the package inside, but the tail stuck out. The crocodile had decided to straighten it. They used their force to bend the tail so that it could fit in the trunk. This was not easy, but they managed to shut the trunk, and that was it.

My driver, Djima, and I entered the car and drove off immediately. The drive took about an hour because we had to drive through the traffic in town. When we arrived at the gates of the sanctuary, the sun was about to set. The lake reflected the colors of the sky, which was turning orange. We were received by a small group of people. They seemed to know just by looking at the car that we were the party that was carrying the crocodile. They positioned themselves strategically, and as the trunk opened, they grabbed the prized package, carried it out, and placed it on the ground. Then, they quickly took off the jute wrap on the head of the crocodile to verify that, indeed, it was a crocodile and not some other creature such as a dinosaur.

And they were happy with what they saw. They said that it was a very nice and strong young male. Before we could say anything further, they took the fellow into the sanctuary shouting thanks and goodbyes. That was how we got rid of that unforgettable gift. It was such a relief to all of us. We rested for a few minutes in the car before driving back home.

I cannot close this story without answering some questions. Why did Chief Adé drop a huge crocodile in my house? Chief

It Began In Africa

Adé was a tribal chief, a businessman, and a member of the board of directors of the bank where I worked. What would have motivated him to send me a crocodile? I worked in a regional bank with shareholders from across West Africa. The Nigerians were dominant as they controlled the majority shares, although the headquarters of the bank were in Togo. I was wearing two hats. Firstly, I was the CEO of the subsidiary of the bank in Benin, and secondly, I held the office of the CEO of the group that was present at that time in five countries. In my second capacity, I served as a director on the boards of the subsidiaries, including Nigeria. Chief Adé happened to be a board member of both Nigerian bank and Benin bank.

As a professional banker, I always felt a little uncomfortable with the way Chief Adé interacted on the two boards. He made demands that were often contrary to the rules of good governance. I was often the first one on the two boards to speak out and indicate the issues with his requests. Some of his requests would be silly. For example, he would ask for hotel room bookings for additional nights when he visited Benin for board meetings. Or he would ask for extra cars, drivers, etc., while some other demands would constitute a serious disregard for the rules of good governance, such as requests to sponsor his company events, gala dinners, or even push for service contracts with companies connected to him and his family.

Over time, he had identified me to be the main denier of his demands. He used to tell me outside the board meetings to give him a break and stop blocking his path. I used to smile and not say much. Once, he told me, "Please do not step on my toes. You know that my toes are very big." He had also been saying that he would like to give me a gift. He always said that, looking straight into my eyes in an ominous tone.

I would never know what his exact intentions were in delivering a living crocodile to my house that day. But those intentions were not noble. Too bad for him that when he brought the beast, I was not home, and he had to leave it tied to a water pipe. After this incident, when I saw him again a few weeks later, he enquired about his gift. I thanked him for it. I told him that the crocodile and I had become great friends. He could not believe it. He asked me if I still had the crocodile in the house. I assured him that I could not even imagine otherwise. It was a unique and precious gift that I will keep with me forever. He wanted to send me a mafia-like message to intimidate me. It did not work.

CHAPTER 11

SCAMS IN AFRICA

The Nigerian Mail Fraud Story – 1995

The year was 1995. I was based in Benin, and I had just returned from an extended stay in Canada, where I attended an Executive Management Program at the Ivey School of Business, London, Ontario. I have been a member of the Rotary Club in the different cities in Africa where I have lived. However, I have not been a regular at the obligatory weekly meetings due to my busy professional schedule, and during recent years, I have completely given up on the club.

Anyway, following my return after a long absence, I made it a point to show up at one of those meetings just to make a token presence and see some of my good friends who were regular attendees. During the meeting, one person whom I knew as a member and as the head of an accounting firm whispered to me that he would like to have a meeting with me because he had some urgent business to discuss. We will call him Oscar for the sake of this story. We agreed to meet the next day in my office.

Oscar was a senior professional accountant (*expert-comptable* in the French system). He had managed an accounting firm for a long time. He was in his fifties, which meant that he was about fifteen years older than me. I considered him to be an experienced professional. He showed up at the designated hour in my office with a bag full of documents. He told me that he needed my advice on a business that he had been pursuing for the past several months. I requested him to go ahead and tell me all about this business. He began by taking out a bunch of papers from his files and putting them on the table for me to look at. There were a large number of official documents from Nigeria, ranging from foreign exchange allocation applications, bank transfer requests, and letters written by the banks asking for more documents to certifications of safe deposit vaults, notarized deeds about family wealth distribution, etc. He wanted my advice on the banking side. I could gather by looking at the documents that there were large sums of money that he was expecting to receive from his Nigerian counterparts.

As a banker based in West Africa, I was on my guard immediately. But considering that he was such an experienced and educated person, I needed to understand what was really going on. So I asked him to explain to me in more detail how he came about it and what the issue was all about. He hesitated a little, apparently trying to decide where to begin his story. He narrated that he was approached a few months back by the family of deposed Nigerian dictator Ibrahim Babangida. Oscar happened to meet one of the daughters of the ex-dictator at a big cultural ceremony during a trip to Nigeria. She had introduced Oscar to her mother, too. They got along very well, and the daughter, Aisha, told him that she would be visiting Benin soon and would be pleased to see him there again. They exchanged contacts and parted ways.

True to her word, Aisha showed up in Cotonou a few days later and contacted Oscar. She was staying in a nice hotel. They had lunch in a restaurant where she mentioned that over US$50 million that her father had gifted her while in power was held in Nigeria. She wanted to move the funds out of Nigeria. As Oscar was a professional accountant based outside Nigeria, she could trust him and would very much like to have him receive the funds in a designated bank account in trust for her. Of course, for this service, she would be paying him a generous commission (15%

of the sum). She further explained that due to the dissent against her father, it was not possible for her to invest or spend those funds inside Nigeria. Oscar genuinely wanted to help Aisha and also gain handsomely in the bargain. So he agreed to go along.

And he had been going along with it for several months. He was told that converting her money and transferring it abroad was complex. The requirements for these processes kept growing, which became the piles of documents he carried. I noticed from scanning through these files that there have been many attempts at obtaining foreign exchange authorization. Each time, there was a central bank application fee to pay. There were various formalities used to register documents, and new ones kept cropping up. There was a detailed note in the file about the case that was apparently written by a lawyer in Nigeria. It explained the process and concluded that the documentation was now complete and the required approvals would be forthcoming soon.

While I was reading this letter, I could feel that he was looking at me expectantly. When I finished, he quickly asked what I thought. This was a hard question for me, and I weighed my possible answers. Was he asking about the whole deal and its feasibility? In that case, I had to be very careful not to say anything that would hurt his intelligence, professionalism, and dignity. Whereas, if he were only asking about the assessment made by the lawyer about the various steps of the process of authorizations, I could easily give a diplomatic answer. Either way, I chose to take some time and asked him to leave the file with me till the next day. This would allow me to have a clearer view of the situation and give him a more complete answer. He was fine with it.

I wanted to ask if he paid for the various expenses like the central bank fees, registration charges, etc., because they amounted to tens of thousands of dollars. I got my answer without having to ask. He said he had spent a lot of time, money and energy on this deal and thankfully, was now reaching the fruition of his efforts. I asked him to elaborate a little further on this point. He explained that in the last year, he had been working tirelessly to obtain all the required authorizations and approvals.

There had been several ups and downs in the process. Aisha Babangida visited him in Benin a few times, and he had been to Nigeria to follow the process directly. He had been to the headquarters of the Central Bank in Lagos. He had been to Abuja, the capital city, to meet with the concerned federal ministry officials. He was in regular touch with the lawyers who were running the whole process. So far, he had not explained why it was so hard to get the funds released and transferred. Upon my questioning, he explained that the funds were in Nigerian currency and were kept in safe deposits with a security company.

Considering the adverse political climate and the tainted reputation of Aisha's father, the ex-dictator, the authorities had put restrictions on their businesses and financial assets. The funds could only be released through influence paddling and bribes, in addition to all the paperwork. He invested a huge amount of money in these initiatives. In addition to the financial gain that he was expecting, he also felt very strongly about the moral responsibility he had assumed to help Aisha in arranging the release of the funds.

I was beginning to have an overall picture by then. I still had to review the file, but on the surface, it sounded like a very elaborate case of Nigerian mail fraud, or 419, as it is commonly referred to. The number 419 is a reference to the related clause in the Nigerian penal code that deals with this type of fraudulent activity. Certainly, no mail or email was involved in this particular case. Oscar had "accidentally" met Aisha at a party in Nigeria. She visited him regularly in Benin, and he had been to Nigeria several times to see the concerned government departments where the foreign exchange approval and funds release applications were being processed. So, this was a much more elaborate scam than the regular mail frauds that we hear about.

By this time, I had gathered that Oscar was not asking for my opinion or advice about the authenticity of the transaction itself. No. He was fully convinced about the existence of the funds. He was totally certain that he was dealing with the family of the ex-dictator. He wanted to have my opinion, based on my knowledge and experience, on how long this process would take to receive the funds in his account in Benin.

I would have given my opinion on the transaction right there, but I felt that it would be too shocking for him to be told that he had been chasing a ghost all this time. To tell him that the underlying transaction or the existence of funds in itself was highly doubtful would knock him out completely. It was also possible that he may react in anger to defend the deal and outright refuse to consider my opinion. So, I just told him that I had many doubts about the whole process and I would give him my opinion the next day after looking at the file.

Later in the day, I spent some time going through the documents folder. It did not take me long to determine that almost all the documents were fraudulent. Firstly, the receipts of funds by the security deposit company were fake. All the other letterheads, government seals, registration stamps, receipts, and acknowledgments were also fake and based on imaginary processes that did not exist.

I had to see him and tell him about my conclusion. I knew that the hardest part was not telling him that the documents were fake and his chances of making a huge sum of money were zero. It was the part about Aisha that would be the hardest to deal with for Oscar. He had developed an emotional bond with this young lady who was most certainly not the daughter of the ex-dictator of Nigeria.

My apprehensions were correct. When we met again, I began by telling him that the documents purporting to be issued by the central bank and other government agencies were most probably fake. I could see the shock and dismay on his face. He reacted by saying that he had personally met with the officials at the central bank. I told him that in cases of this nature, such meetings were arranged at the highest level, but the people you met were not the real officials of the central bank. The fraudsters could arrange to use certain offices in the official buildings to verify the authenticity of the statements that they made to their victims. He was getting nervous but kept quiet and asked me to continue. And there was more to come. I told him that the existence of the fund worth US$50 million was seriously doubtful.

He could not take it anymore. He stood up and screamed "No!" He could not accept this assessment from me. He would understand that Aisha's Nigerian lawyers may be playing some games with the officials to get some kickbacks, but obviously, the funds were there. He had the proof of security deposits. I replied that security companies could not keep funds in that manner. Their role was limited to the physical movement of funds. No cash transportation company would accept deposits and issue receipts of this nature.

He was speechless now. His mind was working fast and he was reaching the point of understanding Aisha's role in this whole affair. I kept quiet to let the reality sink in. And when it did, he made a crying sound. It was a pitiful sight. His voice was gone. He spoke in whispers. He said that Aisha could not do this to him. She must have been cheated by others. I told him that I was really sorry but he must try to close this matter and put an end to his contact with all concerned persons. He could file a complaint with the Embassy of Nigeria in Benin, but considering the large number of such frauds going on, any chance of recovering the amount of money he had lost would be very remote. Oscar was crestfallen.

I met him again several weeks later. He remained grim about the episode, but he thanked me thoroughly for showing him the light. He confessed that when he had come to see me, he had been asked to pay more money as the release of the funds was imminent. He had not told me that because he could read through my reactions right away, something was not right. He found out that, indeed, Aisha was a part of a criminal gang. Her real name was obviously not Aisha.

General Ibrahim Babangida (my drawing)

"I am you, you are not me": A Story of Stolen Identity – 1998

It was January 1998, and I had completed my assignment in Benin. My next posting was in Abidjan, Côte d'Ivoire, with an international banking group. I had previously lived in that country during the 1980s and enjoyed my stay there, as Abidjan was a much bigger city with a much more interesting and diverse economy in the region, so I was looking forward to this move with great enthusiasm. My role was to develop the group's investment banking activities in West and Central Africa. I was supposed to open an office in Abidjan (for French-speaking countries and another one in Accra, Ghana, to cover the English-speaking countries). It was a working day, but I was at home with movers who had arrived to pack all my personal belongings for transportation to Côte d'Ivoire. This was a stressful exercise.

It Began In Africa

Those who have lived expatriate lives would agree with me that a move from a location where you have lived for several years, set up your home, and built your life is never easy. Moving one's personal effects is a part of that stressful process.

Anyway, I was arguing with the movers about how to arrange my ties and shoes when I received a call from my secretary in Benin. Technically, she was not my secretary anymore because I had handed over the charge of my duties to my successor, but since I was still in the country, she helped me with my move. She asked me if I had my American Express credit card with me. It was a strange question. I took out my wallet and checked. My card was very much in my wallet.

I told her that my card was with me and enquired what seemed to be the problem. She explained that she had just received a phone call from the Air France office in Cotonou. The lady who called was a ticket agent and said, "I work at the Air France sales counters. I have noticed that one of my colleagues is selling a series of air tickets under different names for faraway destinations such as Hong Kong, Indonesia, and Australia. The buyer who is present at the counter is using an American Express card with the name Rizwan Haider. The Air France staff has just received the confirmation from American Express regarding the payment. I know Mr. Haider because he is a friend of my father's, and the person buying the tickets is certainly not him. I think this man has stolen the card."

When I heard this story, I immediately understood that it was a case of a fake credit card. I told the secretary to call back Air France to warn them of credit card fraud and stop the sale of tickets. After this, I consulted with my driver, who was also my adviser on matters involving law and order. He belonged to a family where a lot of people worked in the police and other security agencies. He very quickly took matters into his own hands. He called the nearest police station to report the matter and told me that we must go to the Air France office right away to stop this crime. This is how my driver used to operate. After I left Benin, he moved upwards in his career and became the head of security affairs of the whole bank. Anyway, we headed towards the Air France office. I carried my credit card and passport with me in case they were needed.

Before I left my home, the manager of Air France called and told me that they were trying to stall the process of issuance of tickets in the hope that the police would arrive soon to take matters into their hands. But the concerned individual was getting a bit anxious. He might try to slip out if the police did not arrive soon enough. I assured him that both the police and I were on the way. Obviously, I did not have any authority, but I relied on my driver in this department. When we arrived outside the Air France office, we saw a Caucasian individual walking out of the door, followed by a couple of airline employees who could not stop him. The police had apparently not arrived yet.

My driver made a dramatic turn and brought the car over to the sidewalk outside the airline office to block the passage of the suspected individual, who was completely stunned by the arrival of our car and tried to run in the opposite direction. Right at that moment, the police vehicle made an entry on the scene. The cops clearly noticed the running individual and subdued him in seconds. The station officer of the police was personally present. The manager of Air France also stepped out of the office and greeted the police officer. They spoke to each other and then signaled to us to follow them inside the office. I stepped out of the car and went inside with the police officer, the manager of Air France, and the suspect. The officer asked the manager to lead us to a meeting room so that he could take everyone's statements.

We arrived in a small conference room and sat around a table. The police officer asked us to identify ourselves. The manager of Air France went first and gave his name and position. When it was the suspect's turn, I looked at him closely for the first time. He was clearly a European with blond hair, wearing a pair of glasses that were clear enough to reveal his light grey eyes.

It Began In Africa

He was holding a passport in his hand. He told the police officer that his name was Rizwan Haider, and he worked for a mining company. The officer remained expressionless and motioned towards me to introduce myself. I gave the same name.

At this point, the officer looked at my impersonator, who was at least a head taller than me and gestured to him to explain. The suspect remained adamant. He repeated that his name was Rizwan Haider and extended the passport that he was carrying towards the officer who took it from him. I could see that it was a British passport. The officer opened the passport and looked towards me. The identity photograph in the passport was clearly not mine but of this other person's. He asked for my date and place of birth. Sure enough, the information that I provided matched perfectly with the inscriptions in the passport.

My drawing

This was a surreal moment for me. In spite of obvious facts, I was afraid that I could be denied my own identity. The police officer remained totally emotionless. He asked the suspect what he was doing here in the Air France office. He answered that he was buying tickets for his company staff. The airline manager had a file in his hand that contained all the tickets. He handed it over to the police officer, who asked me the same question. I explained to him that I was at home when I received the call about the fraudulent use of my credit card, which is why I decided to proceed to the airline office.

At this point, I produced my identity papers to the police officer. In addition to my passport and driver's license, I also carried a diplomatic card for being the honorary counsel of Sweden in Benin. At this point, the police officer asked the airline manager about the person who would have called my secretary about the sale of tickets. The manager stepped out of the office to call her in. The police officer asked her what had happened as soon as she walked into the room. She told the same story that she had told the secretary. When she came to the part where she had told the secretary that she knew very well that the person buying the tickets was not Rizwan Haider, the suspect made a sad expression on his face and bowed his head down.

The police officer continued his questioning. After finishing with the airline sales lady, he returned to the suspect and spoke with him with a changed tone. The officer said that it was now obvious beyond reasonable doubt that he had committed an identity theft and engaged in a fraudulent activity. Now, could he provide his real identity and the motives behind his acts? The fellow seemed resigned. He said that he was a Swiss citizen and his real name was Stefan Muller. He spoke in French with a Germanic accent. He looked like he could be from Germany or Switzerland. By now, I thought that the case was quite clear. The police had caught the culprit, and I could go back to packing my neckties and shoes. But the officer continued his questioning. He wanted to know the background and the motives for the act. Who were the people for whom he was buying plane tickets? How would he benefit from this fraud? How did he get a fake credit card and a fake passport?

Stefan Muller tried to give some vague replies. The officer read the names on the air tickets that he had tried to purchase, and they sounded like they were all from Nigeria. Muller confirmed that they were Nigerian. The police officer asked him to empty his pockets and put the contents on the table. He did so reluctantly. He had a wallet and a mobile phone. He was asked to empty the contents of his wallet. He had some CFA francs and some Nigerian currency (naira). He did not carry any other identity document, such as a driver's license. He was asked to explain how and when he arrived in Benin. His fake passport did not carry any entry stamps. He explained that he arrived by road from Nigeria the same day. He had crossed the border with his "friends" without any immigration formality.

I was getting tired of this interrogation. I knew by now what had happened based on my knowledge and experience of this type of fraud. I asked the officer if I could leave now. He requested me to stay a little longer so that he could complete his preliminary inquiry and justify the arrest of this individual who claimed to be a Swiss citizen. I thought that the officer was being very unreasonable, but in fact, he was acting based on his own experience. He did not wish to make an arrest and then receive a phone call from his higher-ups to release the suspect without any further action.

In the conversation that followed, Stefan Muller revealed that he had been trapped by a Nigerian gang who forced him to go to Benin and buy these tickets. They provided him with a fake credit card and made the passport with his photograph that carried my personal data. According to him, those tickets were ordered by some travel agents who would sell them to their clients for real money that would be pocketed and shared. The beauty of this scheme was that the air tickets were real and fully paid for, so the buyers of the tickets could travel normally. Muller would not tell much about how he was caught in this scheme, what he was doing in Nigeria, or where he normally lived. But gradually we found out that he had been used by the fraudsters in Nigeria and this was not for the first time. He had been deployed with fake credit cards and passports to assume different identities and use falsified credit cards. After these statements were made, Muller was taken away under police custody, and I was also able to return to my packing and moving tasks.

One question that remained was why and how they got my details. I found out a little later that a network of this mafia was working with the staff of certain hotels. In my case, I was a regular visitor to Accra, Ghana, where I always stayed in the same hotel. A couple of weeks after the incident of my identity theft, I read in the news that the police in Ghana had discovered a connection between the staff of that hotel and the credit card mafia who would routinely buy credit card and passport information provided by the hotel guests. They even found out that there was a price list for passports of different nationalities.

The hotel staff would simply pass on the information to the mafia for an agreed price. The mafia would then decide which card and related passport to counterfeit and how to use it to maximize revenue. Air tickets were their favorite target for a number of reasons, mainly because the value of the tickets could go very high compared to any other possible purchase. In my case, the total cost of the air tickets that Stefan Muller had tried to buy using my credit card was over US$25,000. Depending upon the spending habits of the legitimate card holder, the credit card company would approve the purchase of the air tickets for relatively higher amounts because this was considered a genuine spending need of the cardholder. Their presence on the airline's premises can also be confirmed during the approval process.

With this kind of money, in theory, one could buy a new car. However, approval of such transactions required many other verifications, including a direct phone confirmation with the cardholder. However, air tickets were easier to get approved for. Certainly, the air tickets scheme required genuine buyers for those air tickets who would pay real money. As long as the mafia could have that part organized, this was a good plan.

Of course, I am talking about 1998. Things have changed a lot since then. We have much more technology, and there are many confirmation methods in place to avoid this kind of fraud. However, as the technology evolves, the fraudsters develop new tools and schemes to overcome the checks and balances. This is an ongoing battle.

CHAPTER 12

A CLOSE ENCOUNTER WITH DISASTER

Crash Landing in Rubber Plantations – 1998

As mentioned in the previous chapter, my second stay in the Côte d'Ivoire began in 1998. I joined the investment banking division of an international bank. My job was to develop business in West and Central Africa. As I was based in Côte d'Ivoire and the opportunities for investment banking transactions were abundant there, I quickly developed a portfolio of syndicated structured trade finance transactions mostly focused on export commodities such as cocoa, coffee, cotton, cashew nuts, and cola nuts.

At one time, I was working on a potential transaction to structure a trade finance facility for the export of rubber and latex. In that connection, I was required to visit a rubber plantation in the southwest of the country. It was about 600 kilometers away, and the road to get there was not in good condition. I was, therefore, reluctant to make that journey.

The plantation company came up with another option. They used to hire a small plane to transport their executives occasionally from Abidjan to the plantations and back. I could take a ride with them to avoid the long and hazardous road trip.

It Began In Africa

I made some inquiries about the aircraft, which was provided by a small air transport company. The aircraft used was a single-engine six-seater Piper. It is supposed to be a very reliable and sturdy aircraft. I agreed to take that flight with the other officers of the plantation company. There were four passengers from that company, in addition to myself and the pilot. We took off from Abidjan airport early in the morning.

It was a quiet and clear day. I was sitting in the second row of the plane. A young finance officer of the company was occupying the seat next to the pilot, who was a talkative Frenchman. He kept telling us about the region and his past experiences of flying in that zone. When he mentioned landing conditions at the destination, I was slightly taken aback. He revealed that it was just a dirt landing strip. There were no ground facilities at all. The pilot was on his own to navigate and land the plane. I have taken similar flights in the past, so it did not really bother me. I had thought that the Côte d'Ivoire had better infrastructure than the other countries in West Africa. In fact, there was an airport in the area, San Pedro, but it was about eighty kilometers from the plantations, and the road from San Pedro to the plantation was a real mess. Therefore, this landing strip was the best option under the circumstances.

The flight took about ninety minutes or so. When the pilot announced that we were going to land soon, I tried to locate our ground destination. But I could not see any landing strip on the ground. All I could see was a thick jungle with some small villages here and there. The aircraft descended to a lower altitude to position for landing. The pilot warned us that he would make a low pass over the landing strip to scare away the random animals, birds, or chickens that may be hanging out there. He would then turn around and come back to actually land, thus avoiding hitting any of those creatures. I laughed with the other passengers on this exotic landing process. True to his words, the pilot made the low (very low) flight over the strip. A number of goats, pigs, hens, and ducks walked off the strip nonchalantly.

Now, we were ready for the real landing. The plane made a circle and returned to the strip. But we did not land. The plane went up again without touching the ground. I was wondering what was going on. Then, I noticed that the pilot was struggling with a lever with his right hand. The purpose of this lever, as it turned out, was to release the landing gear. The pilot was trying to pull out the lever, but it seemed to be stuck. He asked the young accountant next to him to help him out with the gear. The pilot took out a piece of cloth that he wrapped around the lever. He asked the accountant to join hands and pull the level together with their combined strength. While the pilot was working with the passenger, who was now becoming an improvised copilot, the other passengers were getting visibly nervous. Some started to throw loud questions at the pilot. "What's going on?" "What if the landing gear does not come out?" One guy was so nervous that they started to hyperventilate. I tried to calm him down and offered him some water to drink. But he refused my offer.

The plane had, in the meantime, made another circle and was coming back into landing position. The pilot and his "copilot" gave a pull of the lever for the landing gear. It did not budge. The plane missed the landing once again. This time, the pilot announced that the landing gear was indeed fully stuck and would not come out. He would be obliged to make a belly landing of the aircraft, which meant that the body of the plane would come into direct contact with the landing strip. He assured the passengers that he had done this a few times in the past. It would be noisy and bumpy, and most probably, the plane would continue to slide beyond the strip and go into the bush before it stopped.

This was a scary announcement. There was panic among the passengers. The hyperventilating guy had now started to shout abuse in French argot. A couple of passengers were having trouble understanding what the issue was. Others were trying to explain the situation to them. There was fear and anger inside the aircraft. The pilot continued to reassure us that belly landing was a safe maneuver despite the damage to the aircraft and the shock to the passengers. I was preparing myself mentally for serious bodily harm. I was looking at the bushes at the end of the strip. They were more than just bushes. There were big trees, and the land looked a bit rocky. If the plane had not stopped by the bushes right at the end of the strip and continued its push into the wild, then it could have hit something much more damaging. All these thoughts must have quickly passed through my mind.

The pilot lowered the altitude of the plane to prepare to land. He slowed down the engine to the lowest level possible and touched the ground. There was a strange squeaking noise followed by a thunderous roar. The plane seemed to be sliding on the ground on its belly at a crazy speed. The surroundings were blurred by the dust generated. The shock, the pressure, and the movement of the aircraft shook us back and forth within our seats, but our bodies remained tightly restrained by our seatbelts.

In no time, we overpassed the strip, and the plane hit the bushes. The ground after the end of the strip was totally uneven and rocky. The thrust of the aircraft tore the bushes apart, scaring away the various birds and other animals, causing them to fly away in all directions. Bumping noisily over the ground, the plane continued moving from its own thrust. We had forced our entry into the wild nature with such force and noise that this area would have never seen before. We could feel that the wings of the plane were getting beaten by the plants and trees. I was afraid that the plane would break apart and continue to drag us into a pile with serious consequences.

By this time, most passengers were screaming. The pilot, the young accountant, and I were the only people who were relatively quiet. I sensed that the pilot was witnessing the damage to his aircraft. He shouted to us that as soon as the plane stopped, we must jump out and not worry about our belongings. There was a risk of fire. We could already see sparks around the plane caused by the extreme friction.

The plane stopped abruptly. Everything went quiet for a second. The pilot opened the doors and shouted for us to jump out and leave our bags. I had a small computer bag that I managed to hang on to and jumped off the plane. The pilot gathered us all about 200 yards away from the plane and checked the condition of the passengers. It was not a happy sight. Everyone looked panicked and distraught. Some had managed to tear their clothes while jumping off the plane. One fellow was missing a shoe. The pilot waited for the signs of a possible explosion on the plane, but it did not happen, apparently, because the fuel tank was almost empty.

Once the pilot was assured that there was no risk of explosion or fire, he asked us to wait while he went back to the plane and recovered our luggage. He handled this alone and refused any help from passengers. He even found the missing shoe. Our pilot was profoundly sorry for the incident. He kept apologizing to us. But the hyperventilating guy found his voice again and began screaming extremely loudly. He was cursing the pilot, the air transport company, and the plantation company all at once. While he stood there screaming, other passengers collected their bags, and this shocked and tired group of people started what seemed like a long walk back to the dirt strip where the cars that had come to pick us up were waiting on the other end.

We were supposed to return the next day, but the plane was not in the condition to take us back. The transport company arranged for another aircraft, but it would only arrive the next day. We stayed in a beach hotel called La Baie des Sirènes (The Mermaids' Bay). The shock of this crash landing remained with me for a long time. My reaction to such situations is not to panic and lose control. When in the middle of a possible disaster, where I cannot do anything at all, I resign and await what may come. So, to the observers, I seem very composed and strong. This is not totally true. I experience the same feelings as those who lose control.

CHAPTER 13

IT HAPPENS A LOT IN AFRICA

How to Survive a Military Coup – 1999

Côte d'Ivoire was one of the most stable and safe countries in Africa. I lived there first in the 1980s, and then I came back for another assignment to live in Abidjan in early 1998. It was great to be back in this country that, while very familiar to me, had lots of new things to discover, too. The city of Abidjan was modern and chic. The restaurants, cafes, bars, and clubs were sophisticated and stylish. The atmosphere was very diverse and international. There were Europeans (mostly French, but also Italians, Germans, Dutch, and British), Americans, Lebanese (the dominant business community), South Asians of different varieties, and Africans (mostly from Senegal, Benin, Mali, Niger, and Burkina Faso). There was an elaborate seaside lifestyle with boats, beach houses, weekend parties, and beach concerts. Abidjan was a center for African music. Great musicians from Congo to South Africa were often based in Abidjan. There were recording studios that produced music for those artists. Many international organizations had their regional headquarters in Abidjan. This added to the international flavor of the city.

    I planned a family vacation in Cuba for Christmas of 1999. It was the time of the millennium bug scare when the entire world

It Began In Africa

was expecting a major failure of all computer systems worldwide when the clocks hit midnight on December 31, 1999. I followed all the precautions and implemented all the procedures required to avoid or at least reduce the possible impact of the millennium bug before leaving on vacation. We were off to an all-inclusive vacation in a resort hotel in Varadero, Cuba, arranged by a Canadian travel agency. We flew from Toronto on a chartered flight to Havana on December 20, 1999, and arrived in Varadero on a bus that picked us up from the Havana airport.

The resort was great. There were food and drinks everywhere. The beaches were out of this world, with the whitest sand and clearest water that I have ever seen. On the first day by the beach, my daughter lost one of her contact lenses. This would have been a serious problem for the rest of the vacation. I searched for it in the sand desperately and found it in minutes. Thanks to the white sand, the slightly bluish hue of the contact lens stood out discernibly.

On December 24, we were enjoying the sun and the sea when I decided to go back to my room to get some fresh towels and a T-shirt. I asked housekeeping to bring me some towels, and while I waited in my room, I turned on the TV to pass the time. Cuba had no internet and no smartphones at that time. I was just zapping through the channels when something made me stop at the German news channel DW (Deutsche Welle).

What made me stop at this channel was something very odd. I saw the street where I lived in Abidjan. Yes, it would be very odd to see that street on TV in Cuba, for there is nothing special about this cul-de-sac street in the city. But this was not what shocked me. It was what was on my street that took my breath away! There were military tanks and gun-wielding soldiers on my street! What? My German was almost non-existent. But I concentrated on the words that were rolling on the screen. There was no doubt. There had been a military takeover in Côte d'Ivoire.

Côte d'Ivoire became independent from most of the other countries in West Africa in 1960. Since independence until 1994, it was ruled by Félix Houphouët-Boigny. He was a benevolent despot who developed the country substantially. He enjoyed grassroots respect and support until his death in 1994. He was replaced by one of his closest protégés, Henri Konan Bédié. Bédié did not fully comprehend the scope and the role that he was required to play as the president of Côte d'Ivoire. He considered it to be an inheritance that he had received from his successor, who was often suspected to be his biological father. He let the problems fester, and the complaints accumulate. He enjoyed a life of luxury and opulence and ignored the plight of the people. The young military officers addressed a letter of demands to him that he set aside, saying that he would look at them after Christmas and New Year. This provoked the takeover of power by the young officers of the army. They appointed a retired general named Robert Guéï as the new leader of the military junta. General Guéï was my next-door neighbor. He set up his command headquarters in his home. This was the reason that I saw those tanks on my street in Abidjan on TV in Cuba.

Robert Guéï, my next-door neighbor and a retired general who took power in a military coup in 1999 in Côte d'Ivoire

After the holidays, when I returned to Abidjan, things changed a lot. There were armed soldiers everywhere in town, but the mood of the people on the streets remained positive. The new leader had promised to hold free and fair elections quickly without excluding any party or politician. This was a welcome change because the overthrown President Bédié had invented a new code of Ivorian citizenship and had amended the laws to exclude his key opponent and the past prime minister during the rule of Houphouët-Boigny, Alhassane Ouattara because he came from a family that originated in Burkina Faso.

The public euphoria about the new regime did not last very long. General Guéï, who had promised not to be a candidate in the next election, changed his mind and ran for the position. Not only this, but he also barred the two main opponents, Konan Bédié and Alhassane Ouattara, from participating in the elections. He made a deal with minority leader Laurent Gbagbo, whose party agreed to participate in the elections. The deal was that General Guéï would be elected president, and he would name Laurent Gbagbo as his prime minister. Most international organizations and election observers decided to stay away from these elections, although they regarded them as unfair because of the exclusion of the two main politicians and political parties of the country. Laurent Gbagbo had assured the General of the desired results. He had been a leader of the teachers' union of Côte d'Ivoire for many years and enjoyed considerable influence over the leadership of the union.

Since the polling stations were set up in schools around the country and the teachers were responsible for voting and compilation of results, Laurent Gbagbo was in a very strong position to obtain the results of his liking. As the main parties boycotted the election and the international community withdrew from any monitoring of the electoral process, Laurent Gbagbo took it upon himself to determine the outcome of the elections. On the polling day (October 22, 2000), the voting booths remained empty. Only 12% of the registered voters cast their votes.

The General was waiting for the results to be announced on television so that he could start his victory celebration. But he was in for a big surprise. Laurent Gbagbo had played a double game with him. When the results were announced, Laurent Gbagbo was declared the winner and the next president of the country. This was a total shock to the General. He kept asking for Laurent Gbagbo to come and see him, but instead of showing up at the General's headquarters, as he did almost every day in the past, he sent out his party workers in the street to demand the handover of power to the newly elected president.

As I mentioned earlier, I lived next door to the General. After the military takeover, it became very hard to live in that house because of what my street had become. It was a barricaded military base with armored cars and soldiers who would check everyone entering the street. I was thinking of leaving this house and renting another place somewhere more peaceful. And one event made me change my residence ASAP.

One Saturday morning, I was getting ready to go to my office (I have always worked on Saturday mornings in my office as I found it very peaceful and productive) when my cook Marcellin knocked on my bedroom door. I opened the door and asked him what the matter was. He told me that some soldiers were here to see me. I asked if they were inside the house, and he said yes, they were in the living room. I walked to my living room to see not one or two but over 30 armed soldiers sitting or standing in various combat positions. One of them had taken a seat on the dining table. He greeted me and asked me to sit near him. He then explained that they had received some information about me and they had come to search my residence.

The night before, I had seen on national television one senior military officer who was telling the viewers that they must ask for a signed official search warrant if anyone comes to their home or business to conduct a search. Based on this knowledge,

It Began In Africa

I asked if they had a search warrant. He replied that they did not have the warrant, but they had these. And he pointed towards his automatic rifle. As if on cue, several other soldiers in the room made the signature motion of pointing to their guns. I had to agree that, in that case, they may proceed. The soldiers went to work in my house. They left no stone nor cupboards, drawers, wardrobes, suitcases, or boxes unturned. They went through everything in my home in detail. They took notes of what they saw. They thought that I had too many suits and ties.

At one point, their chief asked me how I could be so patient and calm. I told him that the reason for me being calm was that I was alone in my house. My daughters had returned to Canada a few days ago. I would not have been so calm if my daughters were home. They shook their heads and agreed that it made sense. After having gone through the entire house, checking every square inch of the space, including the kitchen (they thought I had too many spices), and making detailed notes of what was found, they sat down again in the living room and wrote down a report. It took them a long time to finish their report.

At the end of the report, they needed to write my name, address, and identity card details. So, I handed them my resident card. They looked at it with a strange expression on their faces. They seemed to be surprised. I asked them if everything was okay. To respond to me, the chief cleared his throat and said, "We received reports that you were a Lebanese arms dealer. You rented this house to have a very clear and direct view of the house of the General. According to those reports, you were waiting for the instructions to assassinate the General from your balcony. It appears that you are not that person. You are just a banker. We don't waste our time on bankers." Their grave demeanor and combative postures had suddenly disappeared.

I told them that if they had asked about my background and identity in the beginning, I would have told them right away. But since they had taken me to gunpoint, I let them do what they wanted. The chief felt embarrassed. He quietly completed the report and asked me to sign it. I quickly went through the several pages of inventory of my personal belongings that they had listed in that report, including the brands of my ties and shoes, and signed it with a smile. They gave me a carbon copy of the report and got up to leave. I asked them if their inquiry was over or if there was going to be some follow-up to this search. They did not know what to say. The chief just said that he found me to be a very calm and polite man who did not even offer them a cup of coffee. They just laughed at this final remark and left the house. After their departure, my living room did not look normal again. I could not look at my living room without the thought of those 30 fully armed soldiers occupying it.

Soon after this event, I found another house in a different neighborhood across the lagoon. My stay in Côte d'Ivoire came to an end in July 2021 when I resigned from my job and joined the same regional bank in Togo where I had worked earlier.

CHAPTER 14

I NEED A MAP

Are We in Africa?

Everyone says that Africa is a very diverse continent. The worldwide web will tell you that Africa is a continent renowned for its remarkable geographical diversity, encompassing a vast array of landscapes, ecosystems, and climatic zones. From the expansive Sahara Desert in the north, stretching across numerous countries, to the lush rainforests of Central Africa, the continent showcases a striking dichotomy of environments. The Great Rift Valley, a geological wonder, traverses the eastern part of the continent, giving rise to impressive escarpments, lakes, and volcanic peaks.

Southern Africa boasts a diverse topography, with the arid expanse of the Kalahari Desert juxtaposed against the iconic table mountains of the Cape. The mighty Nile River, the longest in the world, winds its way through northeastern Africa, sustaining civilizations along its course. The rich biodiversity of Africa is reflected in its savannas, home to iconic wildlife such as elephants, lions, and giraffes. This geographical mosaic not only contributes to the continent's natural beauty but also plays a crucial role in shaping the diverse cultures and societies that call Africa home.

Do the people who live in Africa think that they are living in Africa? Do they consider themselves to be African? Aha! This is truly a sensitive subject. Most Africans do acknowledge that they are African, and they live on the continent of Africa, but a large number (tens of millions of people) either do not believe that their homeland is in Africa, or they don't think that they are themselves Africans or both.

You will probably ask how that is possible. To elaborate, I will tell you a couple of very short stories.

The first story is a phone conversation I had with my boss' secretary in 1999. I was based in Abidjan, working in the investment banking division of an international bank. The bank had recently opened offices in Johannesburg, South Africa, and my boss, who was the president of the subsidiary for Africa, was based there. He moved from London, UK, to be closer to the markets that he was responsible for. I had made a call to speak to him, something that I would routinely do. This time, his secretary answered.

Me: "Hello, Ingrid, this is Rizwan. How are you? Can I speak to Frank (my boss)?"

Secretary: "Hi Rizwan, I am fine, thanks. Listen, Frank is away. He is traveling in Africa."

Me: "I see. He is traveling in Africa. And you, Ingrid, where are you traveling?"

Secretary: "Me? I am right here. I am not traveling anywhere."

Me: "All right. So where are you exactly?"

Secretary: "Oh, Rizwan, you know I am in Joburg."

Me: "Right. Where is Joburg?"

Secretary: "Come on, Rizwan. Joburg is in South Africa! Why are you doing this?"

Me: "South Africa, is it? Ah! South AFRICA! It means that you are in Africa. And Frank is also traveling in Africa. Could this mean that both of you happen to be on the same continent?"

At this point, she realized where I was going. She was a white South African. She had grown up with the idea that Africa was a place that was clearly separate from South Africa. She was not alone in thinking along these lines. Many people continue to have this misconception.

The second story took place during a visit to Cairo, Egypt, where I was attending a large conference. I was based in Côte d'Ivoire and had traveled there from Abidjan. During the meetings and receptions, when I introduced myself and exchanged business cards, people would invariably say, "Oh, you have come from Africa!" I found it quite amusing and would answer along these lines, "No. I traveled within Africa. I am still in Africa. Are you somewhere else?" This would provoke all kinds of reactions. Some people would realize the irony and laugh. Others would not get my point at all. They would say things like: "Yes, yes, you traveled from Africa to Egypt," or "I am in Egypt, of course."

There are several countries in Africa where a large number of people either do not quite feel that they are a part of Africa or they think that somehow the real Africa is somewhere else. Those countries include South Africa, Egypt, Ethiopia, Algeria, Tunisia, the islands of Cape Verde, Zanzibar, and Madagascar. They talk about Africa and Africans as if they somehow do not belong to either of them.

In addition to this phenomenon, there are, of course, the ethnic communities long settled in Africa, coming from other parts of the world, such as the Indian subcontinent, Lebanon, Syria, Greece, Britain, France, Portugal, Germany, Spain, China, Indonesia, Malaysia, etc. These communities conserve their cultural and linguistic identities to varying degrees. Often, they are not considered African even if they carry the papers to prove it.

Today, some fifty-four countries in Africa are generally recognized. This list does not include the Republic of Western Sahara and Somaliland, which are not recognized by the international community. The map of Africa was drawn and redrawn frequently by the various European colonial powers (Britain, France, Belgium, Portugal, Spain, Italy, and Germany).

It Began In Africa

In 1914, when World War I began, the map of Africa looked like this:

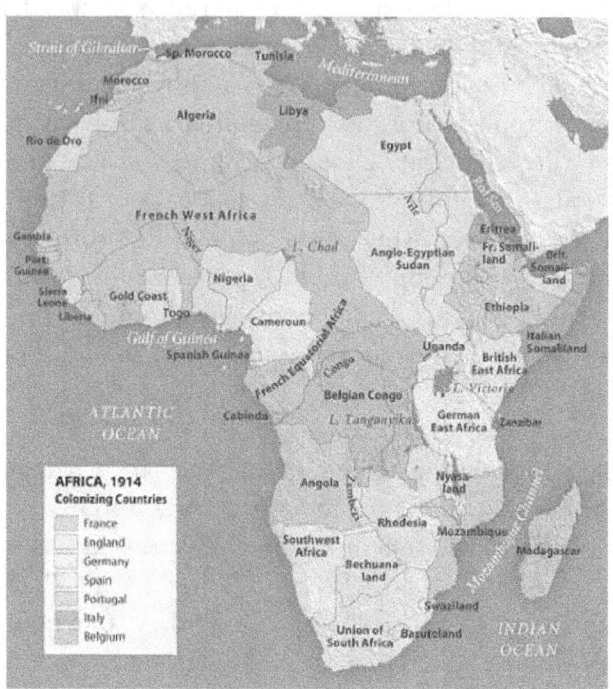

At that time, there were only two independent states in Africa, namely, Liberia and Ethiopia. After the two World Wars, the European colonial powers withdrew from Africa, and a large number of countries appeared on the map. However, it may seem that at some point, they ran out of names to give to the newly independent countries. Therefore, we happen to have the following situation:

1. We have two countries named Congo. They are identified by adding the names of their capital cities: Congo-Brazza(ville) and Congo-Kinshasa. The latter was renamed "Zaire" for a while (from 1965 to 1997). When the famous boxing match between Mohammad Ali and Georges Foreman took place

in Kinshasa (1974), the country was called Zaire. This did help many to distinguish it from the other Congo. But apparently, simplification was not in the cards. So, the country reverted to the name "Congo" in 1997.
2. We have three Guineas: The larger Guinea is referred to as Guinea-Conakry, adding the name of its capital. It is an ex-French colony. Then there is Guinea-Bissau, an ex-Portuguese colony in West Africa. The third Guinea is in Central Africa. It is called Equatorial Guinea, an ex-Spanish colony.

Having lived in Africa for decades and having traveled within the continent extensively, it is obvious to me that most of the borders of African countries were drawn arbitrarily by the colonial powers either for their administrative reasons or as a result of negotiations and compromises with other colonial countries. At the time of the independence of a large number of African countries (1960), the borders drawn by the then-colonial masters were made permanent. The newly independent countries decided not to get into the extremely cumbersome process of redefining the borders. Therefore, the current borders of African countries are often arbitrary and absurd.

CHAPTER 15

CANADA DISCOVERS ANGOLA

First Canadian Delegation – 2006

The Angolan Civil War began when various political groups fought against the colonial power (Portugal) for independence. The country became independent in 1975. However, immediately after independence, fighting broke out between the pro-Soviet (socialist) group People's Movement for Liberation of Angola (MPLA) and the pro-West National Union for Total Independence of Angola (UNITA). This is the abbreviated version of history, in any case.

Now, when the civil war finally came to an end in 2002, the winner was the MPLA, which had been backed both financially and militarily by the Soviet bloc, including Cuba. Their opponent, the UNITA of Jonas Savimbi, had been financed, armed, and equipped for decades by the Western powers, including the white minority regime of South Africa. Since José Eduardo Dos Santos of MPLA had defeated the UNITA, he embarked upon the process of reconstruction of the country that was devastated by prolonged civil conflicts. He asked for international assistance. The response from the Western countries was underwhelming, to say the least, because they were unhappy about the loss of their ally Savimbi. So, he moved towards China, and China responded enthusiastically with a series of agreements and deals.

As it happens, Angola is endowed with massive natural resources, including oil, diamonds, gold, and many other mineral deposits. So, the reluctance of Western countries to come to the help of Angola did not last very long. Mining companies from Australia, Canada, the US, Brazil, and the European Union were keen to enter Angola to take advantage of the mining opportunities. They impressed upon their respective governments to open business and investment relations with Angola to compete with China, Brazil, and Russia, who were gaining ground and winning exploration and exploitation contracts there.

In 2006, I was working at a Canadian federal government corporation responsible for the promotion and support of Canadian exports and investments abroad. I had a specific responsibility for the African continent. The interested Canadian companies were organized under an association that operated with the support of the Federal Ministry of Foreign Affairs and the main foreign aid agency. This group had been trying to lead a delegation of Canadian companies and government officials to Angola to jumpstart trade and investments. One of the key reasons for their lack of success so far was their inability to book hotel rooms for the members of the delegation in the capital city of Angola, Luanda. I could not believe that such a flimsy excuse could stall a major country initiative.

I had just returned from a trip to East Africa when this was being discussed. I had no direct links in Angola, but I spoke with someone who worked for a top international accounting firm whom I met on my recent trip to Nairobi, Kenya. This person told me that she had been transferred to their office in Angola and would soon be leaving for Luanda. I told myself that I must try to get some leads about the hotel booking situation in Angola through her. I managed to contact her, and she connected me with a public relations firm based in Luanda that was run by a Portuguese lady. I spoke with this lady who spoke good English and told me how things were done in Angola with regard to the hotels.

Learning about the hotel booking situation in Luanda was quite an eye-opener. She explained that there were only two "decent" hotels operating in Luanda for business travelers. Both were owned by the same company. That was not too surprising, but she went on to inform me that the reason why the hotels always show as fully booked is because they are officially booked year in and year out by the international oil companies operating in Angola. They don't always physically occupy all rooms. Far from that, more than half of the rooms in the two hotels are not occupied, although they are booked and paid for by those oil companies. The hotel management takes advantage of this situation and sublets those rooms to other clients. However, these second bookings are made unofficially, so they do not confirm anything by email or online. It could only be done through reliable parties on the spot. This explained why our Canadians could not book a room for over two years.

Of course, the PR firm where this Portuguese lady worked could get the hotel bookings for the Canadian delegation for a fee. Now, I had to convince the Canadian federal government and the top Canadian corporations that they should trust the hotel booking confirmations issued not by the hotels but by this lady, let us call her Isabel. The chairman of the association, in his Quebec-accented French, asked me if I wanted the entire Canadian establishment to blindly follow this lady and arrive with a delegation of 40 people in the chaotic town of Luanda without an official hotel booking. I replied, "Yes, this is exactly what I am suggesting." Surprisingly, he accepted my word and went on to put together the delegation. We signed a contract with Isabel and got our hotel bookings "confirmed" by her.

It Began In Africa

Trillions of dollars and Nelly Furtado

Another interesting point to note here is that there was no Canadian embassy in Angola. The embassy that took care of the Canadian interests in Angola was based in Harare, Zimbabwe. One cannot overemphasize how completely impractical this arrangement was. Zimbabwe was going through deep economic, monetary, and political turmoil. The country was mostly at a standstill due to a complete collapse of its currency, the mighty Zimbabwean dollar. The rate of exchange of the currency to the US dollar had reached trillions for one US dollar.

A Zimbabwean currency note during hyperinflation

The Canadian ambassador and a small staff lived in a beautiful compound in Harare and just waited for things to improve. They had hardly any interest in Angola. They had already advised that traveling to Angola was not feasible. Our "bookings" also included accommodation for the Canadian ambassador who arrived in Luanda on the same flight as the rest of the delegation. We all connected in Johannesburg and landed together in Luanda. We were greeted by Isabel at the airport. The ambassador wanted to take control and show some leadership, so she asked the chairman of the association and me about the hotel bookings, appointments, meetings, seminars, etc., that were supposed to constitute the activities of the delegation.

Both the chairman and I kept pointing towards Isabel in our replies as she was supposed to be taking care of all those arrangements. The ambassador was unimpressed by all this. She directly asked Isabel who she was. And here I got an early taste of what was going to follow. Isabel replied with a straight face, "I am Nelly Furtado."

This did not go down well with the ambassador. I tried to defuse the situation and quickly explained the arrangements to the ambassador. When Isabel uttered this phrase, the members of the delegation including myself could see a resemblance between her and the famous singer. But everyone kept quiet to change the subject and reduce the tension. I told the ambassador how Isabel was instrumental in our hotel bookings and other logistics and appointments.

Later on, we were able to carry out the delegation activities reasonably well despite the challenges that everyone had to face in the city of Luanda. For example, the hotel rooms were available at a very steep price. The nightly rate was about US$500, an astronomical sum for those working in the Canadian government. I had to explain this price to the accounts department upon my return. The accountants concluded that I was a big international spender living in opulent luxury.

But in reality, contrary to the wild imagination of the accountants, was there opulence or only regular luxury in the hotel? For starters, the rooms were just basic, and to top it all off, there was no notion of service from the hotel staff. They never looked at the clients. You could talk to them in English or broken Portuguese as much as you wanted, and they would show little or no reaction.

The worst part was the coffee shop experience. The hotel had a proper restaurant, but it was always booked in advance by outside clients and was very expensive. All hotel residents generally had their meals in the coffee shop unless they were courageous enough to venture out into town to a restaurant outside the hotel. Our delegation would leave the hotel in the morning for our meetings and appointments after a struggle to get some breakfast. Mostly, it was a cup of coffee and a piece of bread. The orders took forever.

So, after waiting for a while, one would just grab a coffee and go. The evening meal was trickier. When I returned to the hotel after a whole day of meetings and the nightmarish traffic jams of Luanda, I just wanted to have a quick meal before going up to my room. But it was not so easy. The simplest item to order was a Portuguese sandwich called Prego.

Prego Sandwich, image from Portuguese Recipes
https://www.portugueserecipes.com.

It was simply a bun with a slice of roast beef inside. It was not bad at all. The meat was tender, and the bread was tasty. You would catch hold of a server and place your order, and he would first serve you whatever drink you ordered. And then he would not be traceable for the foreseeable future. The way the service functioned (or did not function) was that each order was personally handled by a specific server. You could not talk to any other server if you could not find the one who took your order.

During my visits to Angola—and these visits became frequent as the business opportunities for Canadian companies began to multiply—it happened more than once that I ordered my sandwich with a drink, ended up having my drink without any food, and retired to my room exhausted and hungry.

Motorola sandwich

Here, it is important to mention another type of sandwich that was sold on the streets of Luanda. It was called the Motorola sandwich. I heard Angolans mention this sandwich, but my Portuguese was limited, and I could not fully grasp what they were talking about. Obviously, I asked our guide to all things Angola, Isabel, aka Nelly Furtado. She explained that "Early mobile phones that appeared in Angola were from the Motorola Company. These phones had an antenna sticking out. The sandwich existed before the phones arrived. However, the name was so hilariously adequate that everyone forgot what the sandwich was called previously. It is a chicken leg between two pieces of bread with the chicken bone sticking out like an antenna!"

Motorola sandwich (my illustration)

My Boss Visits Angola with Me

Once the business flow with Angola had been established, my boss, who headed the international business group, expressed an interest in visiting Angola. I checked with his assistant if he had ever visited Africa in the past. She told me that the boss had never set foot on African soil. This was not going to be easy. Angola was not the country that you visited with your boss, who had no past experience traveling in Africa.

It Began In Africa

Before the travel arrangements started, I had a quick meeting with him. I tried to explain to him that maybe for his first visit, he may go to Egypt, Algeria, Morocco, South Africa, Kenya, Côte d'Ivoire, or any such traveler-friendly country to get some idea of what it was like and what the challenges were. But he had other stuff on his mind. He was really excited about some agreements and memorandums of understanding that he would be signing during his trip to Angola.

So, the travel department made the arrangements. We had to get visas, hotel bookings, and air tickets. I insisted that we take the most direct route. When I traveled to Africa, I covered about three countries in each trip. I would take a flight from Montreal to Paris and then Paris to Johannesburg. I used Johannesburg as the starting point to connect to other countries in the Southern and Eastern zones.

But to travel with my boss, we decided to take a British Airways flight from Ottawa to London and then a connecting flight to Luanda. This way, we would arrive in Angola in the morning. Somehow, things looked better for a first-timer to Angola when the sun was shining as opposed to the darkness of a tropical night with limited street lights and heavy traffic.

We arrived in London on time and, after a short layover, boarded our flight to Luanda. We were enjoying a drink before the take-off when the pilot announced that due to a technical issue, all passengers must disembark and wait in the lounge until the problem was sorted out. My boss was not amused. We deplaned and settled in the lounge to wait for further instructions. A couple of hours passed by without any news. Finally, after the passengers became restless, it was announced that the flight was being canceled. All passengers were to proceed to hotels for an overnight stay as departure was rescheduled for the next morning.

All this was not going well with my boss. He did not say much and followed the process. We were bused back to the departure lounge at dawn the next morning and began the wait to board the plane. We had to wait for a few more hours. The flight was uneventful, and my boss began to relax.

When the plane landed at Luanda airport, night had fallen on the city. The sky was covered by thick clouds. One could see lightning on the horizon. We disembarked and lined up for the immigration processes. I noticed that there were many American oil industry workers on the plane. While we awaited our turn to get our passports stamped, thunder roared over the flimsy roofs of the airport building, followed by a massive rainfall. Before we could grasp the situation, all the lights went out. Now, we were standing in a pitch-dark space, with a thunderstorm raging in its full splendor over us.

After an initial series of sounds of disappointment made by the travelers, there was complete silence. People started to turn on the flashlights on their mobile phones. It was a weird show of flashlights moving in all directions without illuminating much. It was at this point that a group of oil workers, most probably from the state of Georgia in the US, broke into a gospel song. "I love you, my Lord; oh, your mercy never fails…"

It was a strange moment. Nobody could tell where we were. We were transported to another dimension. This is when my boss spoke to me. He said: "Rizwan, where have you brought me? What is this place?"

Gospel singing at Luanda airport under power failure (my drawing)

It Began In Africa

Luckily, the power was restored within the next twenty minutes or so, and we were transported back to the reality of the immigration counters at Luanda airport. The rest of the details of our arrival are not worth recounting, but something happened at the end of our first full day of meetings and appointments. During this trip, our guide to Angola, Isabel, was away from the country. She had set up the hotel bookings, but we were otherwise on our own. I had booked a car and a driver for our visits through the hotel reception. The driver seemed to be a smart young man who spoke a little English, too. He took us around to our various appointments without any problem. At the end of each meeting, I would give him a call on his mobile, and he would wait for us when we walked out of the building.

Our last appointment ended a little after 6:00 p.m. As usual, I gave the driver a call. After a few rings, he answered the phone and said that he was a bit far away. I requested him to please pick us up quickly. The call ended here. I did notice a change in the tone of his voice, but I did not give it a second thought, and the two of us began our wait for the driver. By this time, the day had turned into evening, and the office blocks around us were quickly closing down and turning off their lights. My boss started to look worried. He became very quiet.

I gave another call to the driver. This time, there was no reply. I sent a text message. Nothing. I called a few more times without any success. Now I was also getting worried because there were no visible taxis in this area. There were no homes, shops, or other activities that would bring taxis to this zone. I told my boss that I would try to find a taxi in the area. He said, "Please don't leave me alone here!" Even under the circumstances, I found this hilarious. He is more than a head taller than me and quite solidly built.

I walked a few steps up and saw a couple of security guards. I approached them in my very rudimentary Portuguese to find out if we could somehow get a taxi in the area. They told me point-blank that there was no chance of finding a taxi at that time.

And they asked where we were going. I gave them the name of the hotel. They talked to each other for a while in a local dialect that sounded like Greek to me. One of the guys spoke to me and said that their supervisor would be arriving soon in his van and bringing in other guards who would do the night duty. If we are lucky, the supervisor might give us a lift to our hotel.

The supervisor did turn up in the next fifteen minutes or so. He was driving a small van with five security guys. Our two guards informed the supervisor of our ordeal, and he replied that the guards that he had to pick up would fill up his van, and there would be no space left for the two uninvited guests. At this point, I made him an offer. I said, if you agree to drive the two of us to our hotel and then come back here to pick up your guards, I will compensate you for the favor. This brought a smile on his face. Apparently, he had never had a chance to make a buck renting out the company van in the past. After that, we quickly arrived at the sum to be paid for the service, and he was more than happy to drop us off at the hotel. Of course, he was playing loud music, and we had to bear with that.

I still cannot figure out what happened with our original driver. Why did he walk away without even getting paid for the day? I spoke with the hotel staff who had arranged that driver for us. Though I was not happy with him for parting company with us in that manner, I would still have liked to pay for the earlier part of the day when he drove us to our meetings. The hotel called him over the phone but could not convince him to come and see us the next day. They said he was like that. My boss and I took it philosophically and accepted it as one of the mysteries of Africa.

CHAPTER 16

HE CAME, HE SAW, HE CONQUERED!

Story of a Legendary Mercenary – 2006

It was 2006. I was on a South African Airways flight from Johannesburg to Antananarivo, Madagascar. The person sitting next to me looked unremarkable at first sight except for his height. He was a European in his fifties, wearing a gray safari shirt and cap of the same color. He was probably six and a half feet tall. It was a relatively short flight of about three hours. As we were served the meal, I noticed that he only ate bread and butter.

We began to make small talk as soon as we had boarded the plane, and I noticed that he spoke in English with an accent. He asked me if I had visited Madagascar before and if I knew the resort town of Nosy Be. I told him that I had visited Madagascar several times, but I had never been to Nosy Be. However, during that visit, I did plan to spend a weekend at Nosy Be with some friends. He was pleased to hear this. He told me that he owned a resort hotel in Nosy Be and would be pleased to invite me and my friends for dinner at his resort during my stay there. It was a generous offer that I accepted with thanks, and we exchanged our business cards.

At that time, I was based in Ottawa, Canada, and was working for a Canadian federal government corporation that provided support to Canadian investments and exports abroad. I covered the entire African continent for them. A Canadian company had initiated a major nickel mining project in Madagascar, so my trips to the country were mainly connected to that project. My fellow traveler's business card just mentioned his name and email address. It was a very generic Anglo-Saxon name like John Smith, but I will call him Jean in this story because he sounded very much like a French speaker.

After a while, we switched over to French. Jean told me that he was Belgian and French but now carried a South African passport. He had some business in Johannesburg that obliged him to travel regularly between there and Madagascar. There was something in his mannerism, the roughness of his hands, the fact that he was thin but heavily built with hard facial features, that made me guess that he was either a farmer or a soldier in his earlier life. I casually enquired if he had been in the army. He smiled at my question and told me that he joined the Belgian army when he was eighteen and served there for eight years. I calculated that if he was fifty years old now, it meant that he had left the army at least twenty-four years ago. His service in the army did not seem to explain his physical features.

Anyway, he showed me some pictures of his resort in Nosy Be, and our conversation moved on to the politics of Madagascar and South Africa. He mentioned that he was very grateful for what South Africa had done for him and his family. Naturally, I was curious to find out more.

At that point, Jean asked me if I had heard of Bob Denard. I replied in the affirmative because I had been hearing this name for a long time. During my first stay in Benin (1992–1998), Bob Denard was often mentioned as an enemy of Benin, who attacked Benin with a group of mercenaries arriving on a ship on January 16, 1977. During that period, Benin was a communist country. The attackers were hired by Western powers and their African friends. The Beninese army fought back, but the invaders failed in their mission to overthrow the communist regime. The mercenaries managed to escape on their ship after incurring heavy losses. There is a monument in the city of Cotonou, Benin, that commemorates this event.

The Martyrs Place, Cotonou, Benin

My version of the story of the invasion led by Bob Denard made Jean smile. He said that things are always more complicated than what comes out in public. I asked him if he knew more about the story. He said he could only say that there was strong support for that mission from the political classes of Benin and that the valiant defenders of the Benin regime were mainly the Cuban commandos who were posted there as presidential guards.

Naturally, I asked him how he had such inside knowledge of this event that happened almost thirty years ago.

Bob Denard – A legendary mercenary (my drawing)

Jean shook his head and said that he felt comfortable enough to talk to me a little more openly. He spoke in a low voice. He started by telling me that he had been a close companion of Bob Denard for many years. I asked how he joined Bob Denard's team. He did not want to elaborate, but I gathered that the team was set up with the support of the French authorities. Bob Denard was tasked to carry out various campaigns to implement France's neocolonial plans.

Jean continued to tell me about the various missions that he participated in with Bob Denard. I had read about Bob Denard, but talking to someone who had firsthand knowledge and experience in this regard was, to say the least, incredibly fascinating. He recounted the numerous missions in The Katanga province of Congo, civil wars in Yemen and Biafra, Nigeria, and, of course, the series of actions in Angola and

Mozambique. During the long mercenary career of Bob Denard, he toppled regimes, fought civil wars, rescued trapped forces, disrupted governments, carried out targeted killings, assassinated leaders, took hostages, and collected ransoms across the African continent, in the islands of the Indian Ocean and even on the Arabian Peninsula.

Jean, after two decades of wild mercenary life and many serious injuries and evacuations, fell out with Bob Denard when the latter took a strange move in his already very strange life to take over the island nation of Comoros (Indian Ocean) and became the de facto ruler of that country. Bob Denard did not appreciate Jean's decision to quit his companionship like this. He used his usual tactics, such as sending a death squad to gun him down or blow up his home. But Jean had learned all those tricks of the trade very well.

He survived each of those murder attempts. He had to hide, disguise, and live in fear for quite some time. But he needed real protection. South Africa's apartheid regime had often used the services of Bob Denard for its campaigns to support the pro-Western guerrilla groups in Mozambique and Angola. When the apartheid regime ended in South Africa, the democratic government that took over had no love lost with Bob Denard. Jean managed to contact some people in the South African political circles and arranged to obtain personal protection from Bob Denard. By this time, Bob Denard had begun to lose the soft corner that he always enjoyed with the French authorities. This may be partly due to his persona, which became crazier as he grew older. This was also because more politically correct policy-making was emerging in France.

As the European Union began to act as a political body, it was becoming difficult for France to carry out neocolonial pursuits in its ex-colonies. There was also a generational change taking place in French politics. The younger politicians began to question the murky world of "France – Afrique" that was established by a certain Jacques Foccart. Bob Denard had become an embarrassment for

France. On the complaints from the family of a slain president of Comoros, a legal case was initiated against Bob Denard in France. This was the first time that Denard's misadventures were ever questioned by the French authorities.

The South African authorities offered Jean's testimony in that case, with the condition that the protection provided by the South African government would also be provided by France and extended to the European Union. When I had this conversation with Jean on the plane (in 2006), the legal case was in progress in France. Jean had appeared before the court a few times under very heavy guard and protection. When Jean left Bob Denard, he lived in hiding in Madagascar for a while. He later built a resort hotel in Nosy Be, which became his main activity and business.

He continued telling me the story of Bob Denard until our plane landed. I promised to visit his resort in Nosy Be within a week's time. And indeed, I managed to show up at his resort the next week. He received me with great enthusiasm, as if we were close friends. We had a great dinner, and he continued his story throughout the meal.

I cannot tell the details of those mercenary missions as told by Jean for obvious reasons, but I will provide a brief account of the life and adventures of Bob Denard that are public knowledge.

Robert Denard was born on April 7, 1929, in the Bordeaux region of France. He began his career in the French Navy at the age of sixteen. He served in the French colonial wars in Indochina and Algeria. He was promoted to the rank of quartermaster, but his career with the Navy ended abruptly in 1952 when he was twenty-three years old due to a bar fight in Vietnam. After his discharge from the Navy, he arrived in Morocco, which was a French protectorate. He initially worked as a heavy-duty vehicle driver and then joined the police. Under circumstances that are not very clear, a few years later, he happened to be back in France, where he was charged with a plot to murder then-socialist Prime Minister Pierre Mendes-France. Apparently, the prime minister was trying to end the colonial wars in Algeria and Indochina, and

Denard (and his shady benefactors) did not appreciate this. He was convicted and spent eighteen months in prison.

When he came out, he joined some shady mercenary groups working under the umbrella of French secret services to fight in numerous postcolonial conflicts from Nigeria (Biafra, a war of secession), Yemen (a civil war between traditionalists and socialists), an attack on Dahomey (now Benin), Angola, Congo-Zaire, Comoros and even in Iran. All these fights had a Cold War context, and the belligerents were supported either by the Soviets or by the Western powers. Denard was, most of the time, on the side of the Western powers. Though he operated as a mercenary (a hired gun), his own political leanings were solidly anti-communist.

He fought in Katanga, Congo, in December 1961 when a secessionist movement began, and once again, to support a secessionist President Moise Tshombe in 1963. When things went sour, he moved to the Portuguese colony of Angola. Soon after, he participated in the civil war in Northern Yemen in 1963. Then he returned to Congo and fought Simba rebels in the East of Congo as a part of the French mercenaries called "les affreux." Later, he supported another revolt in Katanga, Congo, in 1966. In 1967, he joined the same rebels in Katanga. He was injured in Bukavo (again on the Eastern front of Congo) and flown to Rhodesia. In 1968, he attacked Katanga with 100 men on bicycles. He was hired by the French secret services to serve in the secessionist war in Biafra (Nigeria) (1968–1978), also known as The Nigerian Civil War.

After these missions, he needed a state cover. So, under the advice of the French, he was recruited by Gabon and moved there as his base for ten years (1968–1978). During this period, he conducted various mercenary actions on behalf of France, including the attacks on Guinea Conakry in 1970 and Benin in 1972. His missions were planned and led by Jacques Foccart, the leading architect of the French neo-colonial strategy in Africa. This strategy was supported by the main heads of the states of the ex-French colonies, such as Gniassingbe Eyadema of Togo, Felix Houphouet-Boigny of Côte d'Ivoire, Omar Bongo of Gabon, and King Hassan of Morocco. He went to Rhodesia to take part in the ongoing civil conflict in 1977 with the support of France, Iran, Nigeria, Zaire, and Comoros.

This last country became his favorite, somehow. He made four separate coup attempts in Comoros under instructions from Jacques Foccart. He overthrew President Ahmad Abdallah in 1975. He came back in 1978 to oust the government of Ali Soilih, who was killed in mysterious circumstances. He then put Ahmad Abdallah (whom he had overthrown earlier) back in the seat of the president. From 1978 to 1989, he ruled over Comoros as the de facto leader with a force of 500 armed men.

During this time, he married a Comorian woman and converted to Islam. He obtained Comorian citizenship under the Muslim name of Saïd Mustapha Mhadjou. While based in Comoros, he was involved in mercenary campaigns in Mozambique and Angola. During this time, he accumulated substantial wealth and property. In 1989, the mostly puppet President Ahmad Abdullah of Comoros, who was concerned that the army was plotting to overthrow him, ordered the 500-strong Bob Denard force to disarm the army.

At that point, a military officer managed to sneak into the presidential palace and assassinate Ahmad Abdallah. He also injured Bob Denard, who was rescued by the French army and flown to South Africa for treatment.

In September 1995, Denard overthrew a newly appointed Comorian president named Said Mohamed. The French government had prior knowledge of his plans, but they did not intervene until he succeeded in toppling the president. However, fearing a strong condemnation by the international community, the French authorities brought in 600 French soldiers to counter him. Surrounded, he negotiated an amnesty for the insurgents before his surrender and preparation for his trial. He later moved to France in the Medoc region. While in France, during the late 1990s, he was tried on charges filed by the family of the assassinated president that he was behind the assassination plot. Nothing much came out of the trial because, under an arrangement with the French authorities, the ex-Comorian president's family decided to withdraw their accusation.

He remarried on May 21, 2005, upon his return to France. However, he was forced to face numerous legal proceedings while dealing with his personal, financial, and health problems. Several journalists tried to meet him a few years before his death to enquire about his life and to write a book about it. At first, he refused to see them, believing that he was capable of writing his memoirs alone, in which he had promised numerous revelations. However, he was gradually overcome by Alzheimer's disease, which confused his memory of past events. His trial barely covered his multiple acts of violence and warfare. He was given a token sentence that was never executed.

He died on October 13, 2007, of a cardiac arrest, taking with him many of his secrets. He is buried in the cemetery of Grayan-et-l'Hôpital, in Gironde.

CHAPTER 17

FRENCH-SPEAKING AFRICA - THE CFA MONETARY ZONE

Myths and Mistakes

I have spent a large part of my life in French-speaking Africa. I have witnessed how, after the independence from France, these countries developed and transformed. The influence of France remained very strong over the region till very recently. The history of post-colonial Francophone Africa is a litany of errors committed by both France and the African leaders, the missed opportunities, and a failure to establish strong and viable economies. In this chapter, I have tried to explain the issues with the monetary system that the region inherited from France and how it has evolved over the decades.

The French colonial empire in Africa came to an end in 1960. The following newly independent states were born as a result:

WEST AFRICA	CENTRAL AFRICA
why Cote d'Ivoire (Côte d'Ivoire)	Cameroun
Dahomey (now Benin)	Central African Republic
Mali	Chad

Mauritania (did not join the monetary union)	Congo-Brazzaville
Niger	Gabon
Senegal	
Togo	
Upper Volta (now Burkina Faso)	
Guinea-Conakry (did not join the monetary union)	

During the following years, Guinea-Bissau, a former Portuguese colony, joined the West African monetary union, whereas Equatorial Guinea, a former Spanish colony, joined the Central African monetary pact.

Most of these countries were small. They had limited economic and financial capacities. The levels of agricultural, industrial, and mineral production were relatively modest. Under those circumstances, the outgoing colonial power (France) decided to leave the existing colonial monetary system intact with some adjustments to account for the status of the newly independent states. During the colonial times, the French authorities had set up a currency in their colonies in Africa in 1945 that was an extension of their own currency, the French Franc. It was called the CFA Franc (Franc des Colonies français d'Afrique). A fixed rate of exchange (1.70 French Francs to one CFA Franc) was put in place by the French monetary authorities to link the African currency to the French Franc. This rate of exchange was adjusted in 1958 when the CFA Franc was revalued to 2 French Francs for one CFA. All the French colonies in Africa became independent in 1960. During the same year, under a monetary reform in France, the French Franc was adjusted by moving two decimal points. The resultant New Franc was equal to 100 old Francs. Therefore, the parity with the CFA was redefined to become 50 CFA Francs, equaling one New French Franc.

Exchange parity with the French Franc

Guinea-Conakry and Mauritania decided to leave the existing monetary union and introduce their own national currencies. All the other newly independent ex-colonies of France assembled under two regional central banks: BCEAO for West African states and BEAC for Central African states. These two central banks began to issue two different brands of CFA Franc but with identical exchange rates that remained pegged to the French Franc. Initially, the headquarters of the two central banks were in Paris but gradually they were moved to Africa. The West African Central Bank (BCEAO) is based in Dakar, Senegal, and the Central African Central Bank is headquartered in Yaoundé, Cameroun. The French Central Bank (La Banque de France) and the French Treasury guaranteed the convertibility and the exchange rate parity of the CFA Franc. This guarantee came with some strings attached. The African central banks were required to keep their foreign currency reserves with the Bank of France. These reserves were not supposed to fall below 50% of the money supply of the two currencies. The Bank of France and the French Treasury were represented on the boards of directors of the two central banks, and there were certain reporting requirements put in place for the two African Banks towards the Bank of France.

The dreaded devaluation

This arrangement has been under a lot of criticism over the decades. However, it is important to note two major events that have shaped this currency. During the late '80s, following a sharp decline in the market prices of the commodities exported by the CFA member countries, it became more and more difficult for certain countries to compete in the international market. CFA Franc was considered to be overvalued for its own good. Pressure grew on the leaders of the member countries, both in West and

Central Africa, to take action to devalue the currency. This was a very tough decision to make.

The key person whose opinion was very important in such matters was the then president of Côte d'Ivoire, Felix Houphouet-Boigny. He agreed on an austerity plan and appointed the governor of the West African central bank, Alhassane Ouattara, to become the prime minister of Côte d'Ivoire to implement that plan. However, he refused to agree to any devaluation of the currency. Therefore, the issue was kept pending. Houphouet-Boigny had been the president of his country since the independence. Prior to that, he was a minister in the French government. He was in his late eighties when he passed away in December 1993. After his death, the French authorities and the concerned African governments decided to move quickly. They announced a 50% devaluation of the currency value on January 11, 1994. This was a major shock to the people across the member countries. The resulting hike in consumer prices, rents, utilities, etc., brought serious hardship to common folks. Strong voices were raised in many countries to put an end to the monetary unions. However, with the help of France, the European Union and the World Bank, measures were put in place to reduce the impact of the currency shock on people with lower income and to boost production and exports to take advantage of the cheaper production costs resulting from the devaluation.

Just before the devaluation, a rift was building up between the two central banks. Central African countries are overwhelmingly dependent on natural resources for their economies. Most of them are producers of petroleum. Others have gold and diamond mines. Most of them are run by despotic regimes with very long-lasting leaders. For example, the president of Cameroun, Paul Biya, has been in his seat since 1982 (forty-one years in power and counting). The president of Gabon, Ali Bongo Ondimba, has been in power since only 2009, but he took over this position when his father died in office after occupying the presidency for forty-two years. The president of Congo-Brazzaville, Denis Sassou-Nguessou, occupied the position for thirteen years (19791992) and, after a break lasting five years, took back his seat in 1997. He has been in office cumulatively for thirty-nine years. In the case of Chad, the current president, Mahamat Deby, has only been in power for the last two years, but he succeeded his father, Idris Deby, who held the post of the president for thirty-one years till his death in an encounter with a rebel group in 2021.

The situation in West Africa is different. Most countries have set up democratic institutions, and governments change regularly. There are of course, exceptions and periods of instability such as right now. Out of the eight member countries of the West African monetary union, three (Burkina Faso, Mali, and Niger) have been subjected to military coups recently that have toppled the civilian regimes and installed army officers in power.

Just before the devaluation of the currency in 1994, the two central banks developed suspicions against each other. There was a mutual feeling that a flight of capital was being tolerated by the other side, among other issues. Therefore, in August 1993, all direct movements of funds between the two central banks were stopped. They also stopped buying each other's currency notes. This prompted the Bank of France to stop buying the currency notes of the two zones when presented for exchange on its counters. This measure by the Bank of France had a serious impact on the most flagrant form of the flight of capital that used to take place simply by individuals traveling with suitcases full of CFA Francs to Europe. Of course, this was not officially allowed, but people with influence and connections in the right places could simply take a Swiss Air flight from their country to Geneva and put the funds at the Swiss banks' branches conveniently open right at the airport. After the devaluation, the divorce between the two central banks has still not been annulled. This remains an inconvenience for the people in both zones.

Replacement of the French Franc by the Euro

The second big event that occurred in the monetary history of the two regions was the end of the French Franc as a currency. Twelve member countries of the European Union managed to introduce their own currency on January 1, 1999. Before this could be achieved, the issue of the parity of the CFA Franc with the French Franc needed to be resolved. The French government, taking into consideration its substantial economic interests and investments in the two zones, decided to extend its guarantee for the convertibility and exchange rate parity to the new European Central Bank. Hence, the CFA Franc was pegged to the Euro without any real change in its foreign exchange value. The conversion rate set by the European Central Bank for French Francs to euros was 6.55957 FF. The same rate was extended to the CFA Franc, and the parity between the CFA and Euro was set up at 655.957 CFA.

Under the arrangement, the relations between the central banks, the French treasury and the Bank of France remained intact. The convertibility of the CFA Franc was extended to the entire eurozone. In fact, other member countries of the eurozone hardly ever noticed that their monetary authority had assumed a historical and colonial arrangement. This change did not have any real impact on the day-to-day lives of the people of the two zones.

The souring of the public opinion about the currency link

The real change was taking place in the way people received information and reacted to it. I am talking about the rise of the Internet and social media. As Facebook, Twitter, and other networks became popular in Africa, discussions about all kinds of subjects multiplied. Over the years, popular opinion has turned against the monetary arrangements between the African countries and France. The general perception is that France has a massive advantage through this system. A lot of people believe that, on the one hand, the currency parity allows French companies to operate in the CFA Franc zone without any foreign exchange risk. On the other hand, the foreign reserves of the zone are held by the French treasury, which makes substantial income by placing these funds to its own advantage. In addition, the presence of French directors on the boards of the central banks and banking commissions provides France with a direct capacity to influence the economic policies of the countries of the zone in its favor. The popular anger on social networks and at various international forums continued to grow. Some populist intellectuals took advantage of the existing bias against the past colonial ruler (France) and made exaggerated claims regarding the supposedly massive money grab that France was seen to be perpetuating over the years. Many such accusers seemed to believe that the French economy was largely dependent on the exploitation of the past colonies.

Although the people with knowledge of the monetary and economic affairs of the CFA zone knew very well that the economic impact of the zone would have been minimal on the French economy, their voices were barely heard by the great majority. The negative propaganda was also assimilated by various political circles in Europe. Certain political movements who were opposed to the policies of France, in general, used exaggerated talking points regarding the monetary arrangements of France in its past colonies in Africa to further their agenda. The French government officials started to worry about the growing negative vibes. They began consultations with the leaders of the countries in the CFA zone to revisit the arrangements and introduce a program that would gradually result in the end of the exchange parity and other related dispositions.

At this stage, it is important to understand that the negative campaign against the CFA Franc has been particularly strong and widespread in West Africa, compared with the Central African Zone. This is partly because West Africa is not exclusively composed of ex-French colonies. There are large ex-British colonies present, such as Nigeria (the most populous country of Africa), Gambia, Ghana, and Sierra Leone. In addition, Liberia (a country established by the US to rehabilitate freed American slaves in 1847) and Cape Verde (an ex-Portuguese colony) are not associated with the French monetary zone. To make things more complicated, there exists a larger grouping of West African countries called ECOWAS (Economic Community of West African States), which is comprised of fifteen countries, including the eight member countries of the CFA zone. This grouping has been running a project to introduce a regional currency for the entire fifteen countries.

The name of the proposed currency is ECO (from the first three letters of the name of the grouping). The project was initiated more than thirty years ago. For the purposes of monetary convergence, the zone has been divided into two sub-groups: the CFA countries and non-CFA countries. The latter are supposed to follow an agenda of economic convergence that already exists in the CFA countries to facilitate the introduction of the new currency. This project has been going on for such a long time and with so little achievement that many observers consider it to be a pipe dream.

Emmanuel Macron (my drawing)

Alassane Ouattara (my drawing)

Under the context presented earlier, the French authorities came up with a series of reforms for the CFA of West Africa that, in the opinion of the experts, would go a long way to appease the public opinion in the CFA Zone in West Africa. The key components of these reforms were the following:

1. CFA Franc would follow a gradual path towards a market-based valuation. The existing exchange rate parity with the Euro would be phased out and replaced by a floating rate that would be loosely linked to a basket of major international currencies.
2. The reserves of the Central Bank of West Africa would no longer be required to be kept with the French treasury. The Central Bank would be free to hold those reserves with central and commercial banks of its choice.
3. France would withdraw its representation on the boards of directors of the Central Bank (BCEAO) and the Banking Commission.
4. The last reform was to change the name of the West African CFA Franc to ECO.

These reforms were announced on December 21, 2019, in Abidjan, Côte d'Ivoire, by the French President Emmanuel Macron and the president of Côte d'Ivoire, Alassane Ouattara, who was also the chairman of ECOWAS at that time. These reforms were signed by the French minister of finance, Bruno Lemaire, with the chairman of the council of ministers of the CFA monetary union, Romuald Wadagni, who is the minister of state for finance of Benin. Alassane Ouattara, before signing the agreement with France, made a quick trip to Abuja, Nigeria, to a hastily convened meeting of the heads of states of ECOWAS countries to get their blessings for the deal. Most of the heads of state participated in the summit online and listened to the chairman, Ouattara, and did not provide any immediate feedback to their chairman. Alassane Ouattara had left Emmanuel Macron waiting for him in Abidjan. So, he quickly returned to Abidjan and made the announcement.

People who know about ECOWAS and the CFA monetary system, including myself, were totally surprised by this announcement. The reform regarding the change of the name of CFA Franc carried a fatal flaw. Everything else did not even concern ECOWAS as the wider body. The reforms announced were entirely an internal affair between the eight member countries of the West African CFA zone and France. However, the issue of the name change was a deal breaker. The new name of the CFA Franc could not be ECO. This was the name chosen by ECOWAS for their future common currency for decades. Only ECOWAS could make such a decision, and no other entity on its behalf could do so. France and the member countries of the CFA zone had no legal right to steal the name of the future ECOWAS common currency. Alassane Ouattara and the French authorities had approved the reforms under the mistaken assumption that since ECOWAS was planning for a gradual introduction of their currency, if the CFA zone announced that they had already adopted ECO as their currency, it would be applauded as a great step forward towards establishing the common ECOWAS currency. Unfortunately, it was not so. The ECOWAS currency was supposed to be established by ECOWAS and managed by a new central bank that was supposed to be set up by ECOWAS. The non-CFA zone countries would never accept that the ex-colonial CFA Franc would become ECO by just changing the name. The negative reaction to the announcements of December 21, 2019, started to grow in the coming days. The council of the finance ministers of ECOWAS held a special meeting in Abuja, Nigeria, and strongly rejected the announcements of Ouattara and Macron.

The French authorities continued the process regardless through the French legislative procedure, and the relevant law was approved by the parliament. Meanwhile, after the position taken by the Council of Ministers of Finance of ECOWAS, the

UEMOA (monetary authority of CFA countries of West Africa) and even the presidents of the CFA countries must have been deeply embarrassed. After all, ECOWAS had challenged the very basis of the "historical" declarations made jointly by French President Macron and Ivorian President Alassane Ouattara. The BCEAO (the central bank for the CFA countries of West Africa) decided to assume a state of complete silence on the issue, and this state of affairs continues till now.

In my opinion, this is the face-palm of the century for both France and its partner states of West Africa. How could the entire French bureaucracy and the diplomatic machine go so wrong about such a basic issue? And how can they go silent afterwards? Even the press in France and in Africa seemed to have forgotten the issue. The press had announced in huge headlines after the declaration of December 21, 2019, that Macron and Ouattara had buried the CFA Franc. The new eco was supposed to replace the old CFA in 2020. After that, nothing. Not a word by anyone. Why doesn't anyone talk about it anymore?

It seems that those who were behind the initiative were so thoroughly ashamed that they wanted to avoid the subject altogether. But what about those activists and academics who have been calling for an end to the CFA Franc? They were unsure how to react to the December 2019 declaration. On the one hand, it appeared to be a move towards the end of CFA Franc. On the other hand, it was very much the continuation of the existing arrangement, with the exchange rate parity and the Euro remaining intact. So, when the Macron-Ouattara declaration faded away, those critics of the CFA remained confused about whether to denounce the declaration or its ineffectiveness.

I attended a conference of African bankers in Paris in June 2019. Some senior officials of the French government who dealt with African affairs were also present at the conference. One such official who worked closely with President Macron and was called Monsieur Afrique (Mr. Africa) of the French presidency made a presentation on the plans that were in the final stages to introduce the reforms of the CFA Franc and the workings of the monetary zone. Following his formal presentation was the question-answer session, where he avoided the question about the consent of the other countries of West Africa who were not members of the CFA zone. But he seemed to be convinced that these reforms and especially the change of the name of the currency would be thoroughly appreciated by those countries. After the formal session, while talking with the participants of the conference, he proudly affirmed, "We owe this reform to them!" I found this conviction and even the premise of this reform both shocking and shaky. I could not see how the idea of giving the CFA Franc the name of a proposed currency that belonged to a different body could be acceptable or feasible.

In hindsight, I can see how the minds of the French bureaucrats had given birth to this idea. The proposals to withdraw their representations on the boards of directors of the central bank and the banking commission and the removal of the requirement to keep foreign reserves of the zone with the French treasury only were reasonable and would have been appreciated by most observers if the idea of the name change were not included in the package. But this is precisely what the French bureaucracy believed to be a masterstroke. They had learned about the initiative of the ECOWAS to introduce a common currency for the fifteen member states called the Eco. They knew that for the purposes of economic policy convergence, the zone was divided into two sub-zones: the existing CFA zone of eight countries,that already had a single currency and a single central bank and a second zone of seven other countries that were not a part of the CFA zone. They had determined that the project to introduce the common currency was not proceeding smoothly. In the past, the CFA zone tried to attract other countries in West Africa and succeeded in adding Guinea-Bissau to its zone. So, the great minds of the French administration thought that they could achieve a dual purpose of firstly, offering the reforms to the functioning of the CFA zone that were being demanded, and secondly, somehow placing the CFA Franc as the common currency of the whole West Africa, just by changing its name. This would mean that management of the new currency would fall into the hands of the BCEAO, the central bank of the CFA zone, which is closely connected to France and the European Union.

Emmanuel Macron and Alassane Ouattara –
They messed up this time.
Image credit: Afrique XXI – https://afriquexxi.info/Franc-CFA-Une-reforme-administrative-pas-monetaire

It was an ill-conceived plan. Here is a list of very important factors that they ignored:

1. The key West African countries with larger economies than the CFA zone, such as Nigeria and Ghana, were expecting to play a central role in the policies, management, and functioning of their proposed currency, the eco. The declaration by Macro and Ouattara that would have given control of their future currency to the BCEAO was utterly unacceptable to them.
2. The French authorities completely ignored the fact that to many Africans, the CFA Franc is considered to be a relic of the colonial era. It represents, to many people, an unwelcome presence of France in the monetary and financial affairs of those West African countries who use CFA Franc. Simply changing the name of the CFA to eco seemed to be an attempt at hijacking the common currency project of ECOWAS by France.
3. This proposal was also a slap in the face of those who had been working for years to make the project of common currency a reality. For those people, it was a purely West African initiative that would be developed and implemented by West Africans. It was not supposed to be a superficially refurbished ex-colonial currency that was deeply connected to France and Europe.
4. The idea undermined the philosophy, the concept, and the process that was behind the common currency project. It also undermined the reaction that would ensue when the reform was announced.

This analysis shows that the present-day government officials of a major European country, with all the modern tools of information, knowledge, expertise, and historical depth at their disposal, can go so catastrophically wrong on an important matter. This is mainly possible because of the traditionally elitist culture of the French bureaucracy. Even during colonial times, the all-powerful bureaucrats of France managed the colonies with meager results. The colonies did not provide the economic advantage to France that was held by other colonial powers, such as Britain, Spain, Portugal, Holland, or Belgium. This was because the decisions by the bureaucracy were based on administrative considerations and not rooted in economic advantages.

France still holds overseas territories in the Caribbean region (Martinique, Guadeloupe), the Atlantic region (St. Martin, St. Barth and St. Pierre & Miquelon), French Polynesia (Society Islands and Marquesas Islands), the Pacific region (Wallis & Futuna and New Caledonia), in South America (French Guiana), in the Indian Ocean (Mayotte and Reunion) and certain territories in the Antarctic zone. They are also a headache for the European Union, which they belong to by virtue of being a part of France. The economic impact of these areas on France is most probably negative. The cost of managing these distant zones is certainly huge. However, the bureaucratic policies that govern these areas do not promote the development of dynamic economic models in those places. They remain dependent on assistance from Metropolitan France for almost everything. Just to provide a couple of examples: The territory of French Guiana, as seen in the map below, is situated on the northeastern coast of South America, bordering Brazil. Brazil is a fast-growing economy with strong agricultural, industrial and mining activities.

However, French Guiana has little trade, investment, or other economic ties with Brazil. Such ties, if they existed, could have developed French Guiana into a vibrant zone. However, French Guiana relies on its relations with mainland France for economic handouts and support. Foreign investment from other countries is also not welcomed by the French administration. So, the area remains economically depressed and lacks any hope for the future. It serves as the site for the launching of the Ariane rocket to send satellites into space, so activities related to this site provide some business to the people of Guiana. But that is all.

It Began In Africa

CHAPTER 18

JOYS OF TRAVELING IN AFRICA

Landing in Lagos When the City Was Shut Down – 2007

Most of the traveling in Africa from one city to another is done by air. There are hardly any train services available. Road travel in Africa can be long and risky, so air travel is often the only option.

There are fifty-four countries in Africa. The airlines that cover these countries are often limited in their means and the number of aircraft available. They also face challenges with regard to repairs and maintenance. Therefore, traveling from country A to country B is not often done on a direct flight. It may involve several connections and stopovers. Most flights are between the airline hub cities and other destinations.

Things often do not work as planned, even in the developed world. There are so many factors that can cause delays, cancellation of flights, or missed connections everywhere in the world. But what happens in Africa is at a different level. We often hear this great explanation offered by airlines for delays in the departure of a flight: "The flight will be delayed due to the late arrival of the aircraft." Of course, this is totally understandable. If the incoming flight is delayed, the outgoing flight cannot

It Began In Africa

leave on time. But who was flying the incoming flight? A crew from some other airline just trying to sabotage our company's stellar record? Or was the flight hijacked by a bunch of lazy birds who took their own sweet time to bring it to this airport? They never provide answers to these questions. This is the situation in countries outside Africa.

When it comes to providing any information or excuses, African airlines have a completely different strategy. They never provide any information at all. The passengers have no choice but to wait until the boarding announcement is made. One can go and ask questions at the information desk—if there is one and someone is sitting there. But the standard reply is that we are waiting for further information. The TV screens often continue to show the original departure times of the flights hours after their scheduled departure time without the departure actually taking place.

I have many such stories of traveling in Africa where things went wrong. But such stories are so common and widespread that I find them boring.

This is a story of arriving in the city of Lagos, Nigeria, which was not a trip within Africa. I was traveling from Ottawa, Canada, to Lagos, Nigeria, on a business trip. I was working for a Canadian firm specializing in providing infrastructure development solutions. On this trip, I was supposed to attend meetings in Lagos and then fly to Abuja, the capital city of Nigeria, for another series of meetings. I had a layover in London followed by a connecting flight. It was an overnight flight from London to Lagos. The arrival time was 9:00 a.m. in Lagos. Everything has gone well on this trip so far.

Just before the landing, the captain announced the weather conditions upon arrival and went on to give some additional information. He told the passengers that Lagos state was holding municipal elections that day. To facilitate the polling, the authorities banned all vehicular traffic during the hours of polling in the state (how this measure facilitated the polling is another subject that we won't deal with here). This meant that all passengers, upon arrival, were supposed to stay at the airport till at least 5:00 p.m.

During those days, Lagos Airport was not the place where you would look forward to spending eight hours. It was a very basic facility, especially for arriving passengers who had no access to any lounge or sitting areas. It was just a long hall with a lot of people who would come to receive or see off travelers. There were some chairs here and there but no air-conditioning or fans.

When I heard this announcement, I felt a deep disappointment. It was a Sunday. My meetings were planned for Monday. I had hoped to reach the hotel quickly, expecting that on a Sunday, there would be much fewer cars on the road. I wanted to hang out by the swimming pool and relax. The idea of spending the whole day at that airport hall was not appealing at all. Anyway, the plane landed. I went through the formalities and cleared my luggage.

With a heavy heart, I walked into that dusty hall where I was supposed to spend the next eight hours or so. It is worth noting here that Lagos is a city that is not for the fainthearted. There are risks for visitors everywhere. So, it was not just the boredom that I was worried about but the risk of losing all of my belongings.

I was looking for a discreet corner with a seat. But I had an eye on the outside, too. In a desperate attempt to find some escape from this situation, I decided to have a look outside. As I rolled my suitcase out of the airport building, I was greeted by a number of young men in the typical Lagos style. "Hullo, Sir! No taxi today." This was not news for me. The hotel where I was staying was not in the main city of Lagos, but just two and a half kilometers from the airport, in the district of Ikeja. I was not sure what I was looking for, but subconsciously, I was trying to find a means of transportation in spite of the traffic being shut down.

The young boys around me were trying to gauge my intentions. One fellow offered me a stay at a nearby guesthouse. While I was listening to his pitch, I heard a jingling of keys

It Began In Africa

behind me. I turned around and saw a tall man in some kind of uniform. He was twirling a bunch of keys in his fingers, one of which was clearly a car key. I observed him walk towards a parked car. I could see an opportunity right there. I walked in quick steps towards this man. When I got close enough, I addressed him in the recently learned Lagos fashion, "Hullo, Sir, can you give me a lift?"

He turned his face towards me with a frown. "You know that the city is closed today," I replied that I knew about the city being shut down, but he seemed able to drive his car. I just wanted to get to the Sheraton Hotel in Ikeja. Now, he looked at me with some interest. He told me that he was an air traffic controller. He had just finished his shift and was going home to sleep. He pointed towards an official-looking paper glued onto his windshield. Due to the nature of his job, he was exempted from the traffic shutdown. After telling me this, he folded his arms and just looked at me. I thanked him for this information and requested a lift again. This time, he smiled and said, "It may cost you something." I assured him that I fully understood and would be happy to compensate him for the inconvenience. He took a few seconds to decide what he would ask for. He asked me if I had US dollars. I said, yes, I did have a few dollars. We agreed on a price of $25. The boys around us were watching this exchange with interest. They helped me load my bags into the trunk of the air traffic controller's car, and I gave them a couple of dollars for their service. One of them told me that I was really lucky to have found a ride like this.

The ride to the hotel was short. There was no traffic on the streets. At a couple of police checkpoints, they looked at the official authorization on the car and let us go. The car had a lot of decorations inside, including religious icons, beads and plastic flowers. The car radio was blasting loud gospel songs. We reached the hotel without any fuss. It was such a great relief for me when the car entered the hotel gates. I thanked the air traffic controller and pulled my luggage into the reception area.

They were not expecting any guests. The reception staff could not believe that I had made it from the airport to the hotel. I told them how I had managed to beat the traffic shutdown. They commended me on my achievement but said that I had taken a big risk. To show their appreciation for my bravery, they gave me the nicest room available.

Had I made a rash decision to take that lift? Was it a dangerous decision on my part? I did not believe so. My experience and knowledge of Africa have taught me that one can often find order in the apparent disorder. This air traffic controller was a trained professional. He was on his way home. He did not propose anything to me. It was I who approached him for a lift. In my mind, the extreme case risk was that he could have sold me to some criminals who would demand ransom payments from my employers. Or he could rob me of my money and personal belongings. Both these risks were too farfetched. Therefore, I decided to go ahead.

For those who may not be familiar with the conditions in Nigeria, particularly in the city of Lagos, it has been considered a high-risk zone for decades. Things have improved somewhat in the last ten years in Lagos but have deteriorated in the rest of the country. Risks of extortion by public officials, mugging, robberies, kidnappings, and car thefts are widespread. It is a mega-city with over 25 million people living there. Urban services and security arrangements are either absent or tend to be chaotic. So, the travel advisories are always very negative for Lagos.

When I worked for an agency of the federal government of Canada and had to travel to Nigeria, it was very restrictive. The first time I arrived with a delegation from Canada to Lagos, we were received by an embassy official and a fleet of cars that were escorted by armored vehicles with guards holding automatic weapons. This whole arrangement seemed to me out of proportion and very hard to deal with. When we arrived at our hotel, the embassy staff told us that for all our outings, either for business appointments or for leisure, we must advise the details to the embassy in advance, and they would send us the armored escort vehicles to accompany us everywhere.

This was totally not feasible for me, during the course of my assignment, I was supposed to visit several banks, financial institutions, and other corporate entities in Lagos. Arriving with this kind of armed contingent would have looked weird and embarrassing. People would laugh at us. It was one thing to receive us from the airport like this, but having the same paraphernalia for each business meeting was just a bit too much to accept.

I took the initiative of speaking with the ambassador and told him that I was sufficiently experienced in doing business in Africa and was conscious of the risks. The armored cars and gun-wielding guards were not necessary for my visits. He was an experienced diplomat and listened to me patiently, eventually agreeing to allow me to move around in town without the armed contingent. But I had to take the full escort arrangement at the end of our trip to go back to the airport. Obviously, I agreed to the offer and thanked him for his understanding. I was very happy to go to my business meetings and dinner appointments just with a car and a driver. This was a great help.

However, at the end of the week, we were supposed to take the return flight on Friday night. The flight to London was scheduled for 11:00 p.m. The embassy advised us that they would pick us up in a van with the regular armed contingent at 5:00 p.m. This was six hours before the flight time. Surely, there was a mistake. It turned out that there was no mistake.

Due to the heavy Friday traffic in Lagos, the embassy had set up a standard policy to leave for the airport that early. The van was fully equipped for a very long ride, with drinks and snacks available. There were even playing cards, checkers, and other board games for our use. Luckily, the ride did not take more than two hours, and we reached the airport at 7:00 p.m. This meant that we would be spending four hours at the airport before the departure time. But the conditions were satisfactory in the departure lounge, which had air-conditioning and more snacks.

A Visit to Congo-Kinshasa (ex-Zaire)

The red dotted line on the Congo River shows the path of the ferry that connects the two cities

It Began In Africa

The year was 1984. I was visiting the smaller Congo (Congo-Brazzaville) for a conference. We reserved a day for sightseeing, but the city of Brazzaville did not offer many sights or sites that we could visit. So, with some other attendees of the conference, we decided to make a day trip to the other Congo. The city of Kinshasa is situated opposite Brazzaville, across the Congo River. This map shows how the two cities are literally next to each other:

During that period, Congo Kinshasa was called Zaire. It was ruled by a charismatic leader named Mobuto-Sese Seko Kuku Ngbendu wa za Banga. This may sound like a long name, but this was not how he was named at birth. His original name was Joseph-Désiré Mobutu. He had taken over the country in an armed coup d'état to overthrow the populist leader Patrice Lumumba, with the support of Western powers, including Belgium (the ex-colonial master), France, and the US. He embarked upon an authenticity drive that included changing the first names of the entire population, changing the name of the country, and adopting a particular dress code. In 1972, he changed his own name from Joseph-Désiré Mobutu to Mobutu Sese Seko Kuku Ngbedu wa za Banga. This is a phrase in Lingala language that translates into: "The all-powerful warrior who, because of his endurance and inflexible will to win, goes from conquest to conquest, leaving fire in his wake."

He was very much in command of the country in 1984 when we made the crossing from Brazzaville to the capital city of Zaire (now Congo Kinshasa). The ferry experience was chaotic, to say the least, with waiting times on both sides of the river for formalities and various payments of fees like government fees. We were a group of four visitors. We hired a taxi and took a tour of the city. The city was built in the nineteenth century by Belgian authorities who ruled the country as the personal property of the King of Belgium. One could see wide streets and a number of colonial-style buildings and churches. Most buildings looked run down and in need of repair.

Mobotu Sese Seko (my drawing)

Things had not been working well in the country for quite some time. However, there was a general feeling of joyous hustle and bustle in spite of economic hardship. There were a lot of people on the streets, and we noticed loud music everywhere. The particular genre of Zaire music that has been very popular across the continent is called the Rhumba. It has a very catchy beat and interesting lyrics in French and Lingala.

After a tour of the city, one American lady in our group expressed her wish to visit the US embassy, where she had a friend. We asked the taxi driver to take us there but did not know the location of the embassy. There was no GPS or Google Maps in those days, so I suggested that we ask a police officer to guide us. The taxi driver was reluctant to talk to the police, but I spotted a female police officer who was guiding the traffic in one corner, and we decided to speak to her. I requested her to indicate the way to the US embassy to our driver. She said no problem and that she could ride with us in the taxi to take us there. We thought that this offer was awfully nice of her. But we were concerned about her current job. She was controlling the traffic, after all. Not that she was making any improvement in the flow of traffic that moved without much order or rules.

When we told her about our concerns, her reply was priceless. She explained that the traffic could manage itself without her. We generally agreed with this statement. She continued to tell us that the tip that we would pay her for the service would be higher than her salary for the whole month. She was not exaggerating or being over-optimistic about the quantum of her tip. The local currency, which was also called Zaire, had depreciated heavily. If we paid her $20 USD ($5 each), that would be almost her monthly salary in local currency at that time.

The police officer managed to share the passenger seat in the front with one of our fellow travelers. She explained the route to the driver and turned on the radio at full volume. The radio was playing a top hit by the famous rhumba band called Zaiko Langa Langa. She explained to us how popular the band was and what the song was about while also pointing to the buildings and monuments on the street. We were suddenly getting loads of information about Kinshasa, its architecture, city monuments, music scene, and, on top of all that, lessons in the Lingala language. Previously, our trip around the city had been rather quiet. Our driver was not a talkative person. He only spoke when we asked a question, and he gave a very short answer. With the arrival of the police lady in the car, an explosion of information was being delivered at a high volume and pitch to beat the radio that was blasting a current hit.

This very noisy taxi ride continued until we reached the US embassy. We settled the agreed gratuity to the police lady and breathed a sigh of relief. We waited until our fellow traveler made her visit to her friend in the embassy. Her friend later invited all of us to have a very late lunch at a local restaurant. The restaurant also played the now-familiar rhumba music. After lunch, it was time to get back to the ferry station and cross the river to return to our hotel in Brazzaville.

A Visit to Equatorial Guinea

Equatorial Guinea is located on the west coast of Africa, with the mainland territory situated between Gabon and Cameroon. The Portuguese were the first Europeans to arrive there in 1472. In the eighteenth century, control over the coastal region shifted between Portugal, Spain, Britain, and France.

In 1827, Britain established a base on Bioko Island (formerly Fernando Po) to try to end the West African slave trade. The mainland portion, known as Rio Muni, became a Spanish protectorate in 1885. Spain had more substantial control by 1900 when the mainland and island regions became united as Spanish Guinea.

During the 1950s and early 1960s, pressure mounted for independence in Africa. Equatorial Guinea gained its independence from Spain in 1968. Francisco Macías Nguema was elected as the country's first president. However, his regime soon became highly oppressive and brutal, leading to thousands of deaths. He was overthrown in 1979 by Teodoro Obiang Nguema Mbasogo, who remains president today after a series of controversial elections over the years.

Although nominally a constitutional democracy since 1991, Equatorial Guinea continues to score very poorly on rankings of corruption and human rights. The economy was traditionally dependent on cocoa production, but the discovery and exploitation of oil in 1995 turned Equatorial Guinea into one of the wealthiest countries in Africa per capita. However, the majority of the population still lives in poverty.

My interaction with Equatorial Guinea has been very limited. During my stay in Gabon (1979-1985), I became aware of the existence of this country. There was a small immigrant community of Equatorial Guineans living in Gabon. They had mostly left the country to escape the brutal regime and the economic hardships. They were called "Equatos" by the Gabonese, which was a derogatory epithet. Many Gabonese thought that "Equatos" were lazy and consumed excessive quantities of beer. At that time, Equatorial Guinea had not discovered petroleum. The economy was mostly based on subsistence farming and fishing. The country, as an ex-colony of Spain, was also isolated as it was surrounded by ex-French colonies who were connected by a monetary and economic union. Equatorial Guinea joined the union in 1983 and adopted the common currency (CFA).

My story takes place in 1981 when the country was disconnected from the world. At that time, they had their own currency, which had been named and renamed a few times as the country went from a Spanish territory to a British protectorate and then to a Spanish colony over a couple of centuries. In 1981, their currency was called Ekuele. They had changed it from Equatorial Guinea Pesetas in 1975. It was not a convertible currency. The bank where I worked in Gabon held an account for the Central Bank of Equatorial Guinea. At that time, they used that account to buy certain products of primary necessity, such as petroleum products, medicine, and some basic equipment from Gabon.

My bank used to send them a monthly statement of their account, but they were having some difficulties reconciling the transactions on their statements. They sent an officer of their bank to Gabon to resolve the issues. I was assigned to work with this officer during his visit. I provided him with copies of all the supporting advice on the transactions recorded on their account. Language was an issue in our communication because they only spoke Spanish (at that time, I did not speak any Spanish at all, nor did anyone else in our bank).

He went back quite satisfied, but later on, we received a Telex from the Central Bank of Equatorial Guinea saying that though they were thankful for the support and documents provided, they would very much want someone from our bank to visit them and help resolve the issues that their accounting and audit departments continued to have with their account with our bank.

When it came to difficult assignments, my bosses had a tendency to designate me to deal with them. Since I was the youngest of the expatriate officers, I was expected to consider the assignments as a learning opportunity and also as a sign of trust that my seniors had in my capabilities. This was how it was presented, but I began to have my doubts about the true nature of why the most complicated matters always ended up on my desk. I was beginning to suspect that I was considered the most gullible and easily convinced to undertake difficult tasks. I kept my apprehensions to myself and agreed to make a visit to Equatorial Guinea.

When I decided to go ahead with the trip, the most immediate issue was finding flights to take me there and, more importantly, bring me back in one piece. There were no regular airlines flying to Equatorial Guinea from Gabon. There were some small planes with six to twelve seats that one could book. But they only flew when they had a sufficient number of seats booked. I made a request to the travel agency that made the bookings and waited for the occasion when I could fly one day and get back the next day.

Luckily, I got an opportunity within the next two weeks to make my trip. The plane was a six-seater. All the other passengers were German researchers who were going on a paleontology expedition. The return flight the next day would bring back another such group that had spent several months in Equatorial Guinea doing their research on ancient animal remains.

I took a flight that departed at 7:00 a.m. and reached the capital city of Malabo, which is situated on an island, whereas the rest of the country is on the mainland of Africa. At that time, the airport was just a small landing strip and a tiny airport building. The flight was uneventful and rather short. Contrary to my expectations, there was no one at the airport to receive me and drive me to the meeting. I managed to find a taxi with a

It Began In Africa

smart driver. He took me straight to the central bank building. I was not told by the central bank about my hotel arrangements, but I was expecting that they would let me know about the accommodation once I arrived there.

On my way, I had my first chance to look at the city. There was hardly any traffic, but the road was bumpy with frequent potholes. The vegetation was out of control, and it seemed as if the equatorial forest was bent on reclaiming the city. The odd constructions were mostly run-down colonial structures. The only building that seemed almost normal was a Catholic church. We arrived at a rather large colonial structure that was as run-down as the other buildings. This was the headquarters of the central bank.

I went inside and managed to find the small office where a couple of other staff members of the central bank were waiting for me. We started the account reconciliation work almost immediately. I noticed that most of the problems were related to language issues and currency conversion problems. They kept their accounting in their local currency (Ekuele), whereas their account in my bank was in CFA Francs. It was replenished by transfers in US dollars that their government made through a foreign account. When I noticed the underlying issue, I offered an alternate conversion and accounting path to handle this in the future. We went through all the outstanding entries and found the causes of differences accordingly. The whole exercise came to a satisfactory conclusion at around 2:30 p.m.

At that point, I was feeling quite hungry and was expecting that they would offer me some food—no such luck. One by one, they thanked me, shook my hand, and walked out. I was left alone to find my way out of the building. Though feeling content with the outcome of the meeting, I was left wondering about my basic human needs, namely, food and shelter. After all, I was required to spend a night in that town as my return flight was set for the next day.

Luckily, my taxi driver had not abandoned me. He was waiting right outside the central bank building. I went to him and asked him to take me to a restaurant and suggested a hotel. Our conversation was not easy as he spoke only Spanish, and I tried French. When he did not follow me, I switched to English. I quickly noticed that he had no knowledge of English. So, I went back to French, thinking that linguistically, Spanish was quite close to French.

In the end, we managed to understand each other. He told me that there was no hotel open in town. This was not an encouraging piece of information. But he took me to a restaurant on a boat that was permanently anchored on the coast. It was late for lunch, but there were still a few people hanging out. The atmosphere was extremely casual. Bare wooden tables and chairs that were nailed to the floor to avoid sliding in case of waves. The owner of the establishment was a middle-aged Spanish man. He came to my table and offered some grilled fish that was caught the same morning. This sounded great, and he spoke some English.

While I was having my lunch, I asked the owner if he could suggest a hotel for me for one night. He smiled at my question. He said that at that moment, there were no hotels open. I did not understand why the hotels would not be open. He explained that due to a complete lack of clients over the last few years, all hotels had shut down one after the other. Having said this, the restaurant owner had a solution for me. He told me that there are four rooms on his boat/restaurant that he rents out. He would be happy to accommodate me there.

I had no other choice but to accept the offer of renting the room on the boat for a night. After lunch, he showed me my room. It was just a bed. There was a common washroom, but I was the only customer, so I had exclusive access to it. There were several mosquito-repellent coils in the room. This was a sign that I would be facing mosquitoes in the night. Still, I decided to take the room.

A mosquito coil (my drawing)

I had a long afternoon/evening to spend. I asked the taxi driver to show me the rest of the town, which turned out to be not very different from what I had seen before: the same overwhelming vegetation and rundown shacks and houses. Before we could make it to the boat/hotel, the sun went down in a second. This is typical of Equatorial sunsets. It does not allow much time for contemplation of colorful sunsets. The city went pitch dark in the few minutes that followed. There were no street lights and very few other lights. It suddenly felt scary to be in that place. The taxi took me back to the boat, where some lanterns were put up to provide some light.

Boat hotel – Malabo, Equatorial Guinea 1981

I got to my room and retired to bed. The slight movement of the stationary boat over the water provided just the right rocking of my cradle. I went to sleep almost immediately. The next morning, I managed to get up early enough to get ready and have coffee before my driver showed up to take me to the airport.

CHAPTER 19

YOUR BUSINESS IS MINE!

Everyone Wants Africa's Natural Resources

Mining for natural resources is a huge activity in Africa. The mining companies include major multinationals from the US, Canada, Australia, Europe, China, Russia, and India, as well as small and medium-sized companies from everywhere, including Africa. In addition, a lot of mining is done informally. For instance, gangs of people who are not officially authorized and are not organized as corporate entities carry out mining without the basic training, equipment, protection, or safety apparatus. The larger mining corporations are often criticized by industry watchdogs, non-governmental organizations (NGOs), and other entities monitoring their

> **Mining in Africa**
> Africa is richly endowed with mineral resources, and mining has been a cornerstone of the continent's economies for centuries. Some major minerals mined across Africa include:
> - **Gold:** Africa accounts for approximately half of the global gold reserves. Major gold mining centers are located in South Africa, Ghana, Tanzania, Mali, and the Democratic Republic of Congo. Gold production involves underground and surface mining techniques.
> - **Diamonds:** Africa supplies over 60% of the world's diamonds, with major production centers in Botswana, Angola, South Africa, and the Democratic Republic of Congo. Diamonds are mined

> from volcanic pipes as well as alluvial deposits, usually through open-pit mining.
> - **Copper:** Major copper mines are situated in Zambia, the Democratic Republic of Congo, and South Africa. Copper occurs in ores like chalcopyrite and bornite and is extracted through surface and underground mining. Concentration and smelting processes produce copper matte, which undergoes electrolytic refining.
> - **Iron Ore:** South Africa holds some of the largest iron ore deposits in the world, concentrated in the Northern Cape Province. Iron content is liberated through various mining techniques before being transported to smelters.
> - **Platinum:** The Bushveld Igneous Complex in South Africa hosts over 75% of global platinum resources. Mining operations employ underground and open cast methods, and platinum occurs alongside other platinum group metals.

activities in African countries. When I began working with the Canadian federal government corporation responsible for support to Canadian exporters and investors abroad, I discovered this very complex ecosystem of miners on the one side and their critics on the other side.

There used to be a Canadian platform of NGOs monitoring mining activities around the world called the Halifax Initiative. As the name suggests, they used to meet annually in the city of Halifax, Nova Scotia, Canada. When I attended this forum for the first time, it was an eye-opener for me in many unexpected ways. I already had a good understanding of issues with mining in Africa that I would have summarized in the following words:

- Many countries in Africa that were rich in natural resources were lacking in good governance and proper oversight of the mining activities. It was widely believed that historically, large corporations exploited African natural resources in connivance with the local authorities. They managed to avoid doing their part in protecting the environment, providing fair employment to the population, and paying the respective governments proper compensation for the natural resources extracted and exported.

- Most African countries with mining activity had performed poorly and remained economically and politically fragile.

However, what I learned through observing the role played by the various NGOs and monitoring groups offered me a new dimension to this whole phenomenon. I discovered that the large number of NGOs active in this field had developed a business model of their own. They were non-profit organizations, but to survive and thrive, they relied on many well thought-out strategies that would ensure that their executives were well paid, traveled in first-class, and lived rather lavishly. The resources that paid for this cost structure came from the consulting activities that these NGOs owned. The way this modus operandi worked unfolded

---

Beyond these major minerals, African countries also mine substantial volumes of aluminum, cobalt, manganese, chromium, uranium, bauxite, titanium, and zinc using both artisanal and industrial-scale mining operations. Oil and gas extraction is also widespread across the continent.

In terms of social and environmental considerations, mining provides employment opportunities and infrastructure development but also impacts pollution impacts and causes resource conflicts in many regions.

Mining activities in Africa have been mired in several controversies over the decades. Some of the major issues that have fueled ongoing debates, concerns, and disputes include:

Environmental degradation: Mining inherently disturbs landscapes and ecosystems, generating pollution that impacts soil, air, and water resources. Most African countries have faced pollution disasters from mining, such as acid mine drainage or heavy metal contamination of rivers. Governments often lack the capacity to monitor compliance.

Community displacement: Local communities are often displaced by mining projects, losing land access or livelihoods without fair compensation. For example, coal mining in Mozambique's Tete province displaced thousands of farmers. Dis-

> putes over land rights and resettlement benefits are common.
>
> **Labor practices:** With many migrant workers and unstable unions, Africa's mining sector has witnessed various labor issues, from health and safety violations to unfair wages and child labor. The deaths of thirty-four miners in South Africa's Marikana massacre spotlighted tensions between communities, companies, and governments.
>
> **Tax evasion:** Groups like Publish What You Pay allege that mining companies use tax havens and accounting loopholes to evade taxes, depriving governments of revenues. Estimates indicate that Africa has lost billions in recent decades due to mining tax avoidance schemes.

before me when I followed the case of a medium-sized Canadian-Australian mining company that had been exploiting copper, cobalt, and silver mines in the Democratic Republic of Congo. This company went through an existential crisis during a civil uprising in the country.

The government of Laurent Désiré-Kabila had heavy-handedly suppressed the uprising. During that time, a video was made public by an NGO, showing trucks with the logos of the concerned mining company, transporting the government forces who could be seen committing flagrant human rights violations. Laurent-Désiré Kabila was a rebel leader himself for decades before overthrowing the regime of Mobutu Sese-Seko. The video served as proof of the active involvement of the mining company in the acts of violence. The mining company had to face several legal cases in the UK and Australia. The company's share value plummeted as the investors and creditors panicked. During one of the meetings of the Halifax forum, I witnessed the persistent attacks that the company had to face from the NGO that had made the video and had brought up the legal suits. The CEO of the company made a very weak defense and tried to explain the circumstances of the incident. He told the forum that the military forces had confiscated their trucks for use in their violent campaign of terror. His delivery seemed lacking in confidence, and he could not answer the avalanche of questions posed by the experts from several NGOs.

I attended the same forum a year later. In one of the main events of the forum, I noticed the same lady who had presented the case against the Canadian-Australian mining company on behalf of an NGO the previous year. This time, she explained how that company had adopted a series of measures to implement a policy of engagement with the Indigenous communities, strengthened the procedures to avoid the recurrence of the events that led to the violent incident, and that now the company was complying with the highest standards of the industry. I was totally taken aback at her change of heart. When I paid more attention to her presentation, I noticed that she was not working for the NGO anymore. She had been assigned as the compliance consultant of the mining company after the past unfortunate events. I could not believe this turn of events. So, I asked the experts and did some research of my own.

It turned out that it was not an unusual occurrence in the ecosystem of the min-

Security concerns: Complicated links between mining and conflict have arisen in the Democratic Republic of Congo's "conflict mineral" trade. Human rights groups say mineral extraction bankrolls armed groups and fuels violence despite regulation attempts.

Corruption risks: Patronage networks and opaque dealings between political elites, government officials, and companies during mining rights allocation have raised corruption allegations. Campaigns to improve transparency around mining contracts, licenses, and revenues seek to combat graft.

As global demand for minerals surges and new African mining frontiers emerge, addressing this complex blend of ethical risks, policy gaps, socio-economic needs, and context-specific dynamics remains an urgent priority for the continent.

Mining in Africa and the Chinese Connection

Any discussion on mining activities in Africa would not be complete without highlighting the growing involvement of China. China has become a major player in mining activities across Africa in recent decades. China needs African mineral resources, especially oil, iron ore, copper, cobalt, and other metals, to fuel its rapid economic growth and industrialization. It imports a significant portion of these resourc-

> es from Africa. Chinese state-owned enterprises have invested billions of dollars in mining operations across Africa. Major countries where they operate include:
> 1. **Democratic Republic of Congo (DRC):** China is the largest foreign investor in the DRC's mining sector. Chinese firms are heavily involved in mining cobalt, copper, and other minerals.
> 2. **Zambia:** China has major mining investments in copper, emerald, and coal mines across Zambia. It is one of the largest foreign investors in Zambia's mining industry.
> 3. **South Africa:** China owns major shares in South Africa's iron ore, manganese, gold, and other mines.
> 4. **Ghana:** China is invested in Ghana's gold mining sector and manganese mining.
> 5. **Guinea-Conakry:** China has mining investments in bauxite, iron ore, gold, and diamond mines in Guinea.
>
> In exchange for mining rights, China provides infrastructure financing and development aid to mining countries in Africa. However, some analysts have been criticized these deals. There are environmental and labor concerns about some Chinese mining operations in Africa in terms of pollution, worker safety, and community relations.

ing industry and its watchdog NGOs. One expert told me that the NGOs would set up very elaborate monitoring and surveillance networks to collect detailed information on mining operations in Africa and elsewhere. This was considered an investment. The expectation would be to collect enough incriminating evidence on any methods and practices of the mining companies. If they could get a real juicy story on a mining company that could make media headlines, then the NGO would expect higher visibility and praise for their work. That would translate into higher donations and grants. Up to here, it seemed to be legitimate and constructive work. But there was more to it. The NGO, through its consulting firms, would then approach the mining company and offer its services to remedy the situation. This would involve a complete compliance audit and a review of operational procedures, contracting methods, hiring practices, community relationship guidelines, and more. The audit and review would not only highlight all the shortcomings and weaknesses but would also present an elaborate action plan to clean up the mess internally and rebuild the image of the company externally.

Typically, such a plan could be spread over several years. And it would cost the mining company a few million dollars. This is how this cycle worked. It reminded me of the pattern that has been highlighted time and again with the US government agencies and major private sector industries that are under their regulatory responsibility. After retirement, government agency officials often joined the same companies that they had regulated as executives or consultants with substantial compensation packages. The situation was even more questionable when it came to defense contracts and the Department of Defense. But that is another story.

The abundant natural resources of Africa attract interest from all corners of the world. There are not many internationally recognized rules and standards that would regulate and

> **The case of DRC and China**
> The Chinese mining companies are active in The Democratic Republic of Congo (DRC). China has engaged in major infrastructure-for-minerals deals with Congo over the past decades as it has looked to Africa for resources to fuel its rapid economic growth.
>
> In 2007, a landmark resources-for-infrastructure contract was signed between state-owned Chinese firms and the Congolese government under President Joseph Kabila. This deal, often called "resources for infrastructure" or "minerals for infrastructure," stipulated that Chinese companies would invest billions of dollars in roads, railways, hospitals, and other critical infrastructure in exchange for access to Congo's vast mineral deposits.
>
> Specifically, the deal outlined a $6 billion resources-for-infrastructure program where Chinese firms would build thousands of kilometers of roads and railway tracks in return for rights to 6.8 million tons annually of copper and 620,000 tons of cobalt. This arrangement was seen as a "win-win," allowing Congo to benefit from trade and transport links while securing China access to vital minerals like cobalt which powers lithium-ion batteries.

> However, the agreement has also faced scrutiny from NGOs and pro-transparency groups regarding debt risks for Congo and fair community access to minerals. Critics argue that China's dominant role borders on shades of neo-colonialism, and caution around high debt loads from opaque Chinese loans echoes criticisms of China's infrastructure lending practices to developing nations worldwide.
>
> Recent shifts have indicated some renegotiation—in 2021, a revised smaller-scale $1.3 billion resources-for-infrastructure deal was announced between Congo and China, adjusting financing terms and focusing on priority road corridors. However, Chinese state-backed firms continue to maintain strong mineral interests across Congo even as geopolitics remain complex.
>
> In summary, while hopes persist around "win-win" infrastructure links supporting development, Congo's expansive minerals-for-infrastructure arrangements with China also create accountability risks that impact economic and social outcomes across the country.

govern the activities of mining companies. Therefore, each African country tries to negotiate its own terms with foreign companies. These deals are not made on a level playing field. The African governments are often desperate to boost their exports and create employment for their people and, therefore, accept such terms and conditions that may rob them of their resources against a low return. The mining activities may also cause collateral damage in the form of environmental disasters and forced displacement of populations. There is a strong need for an international system to regulate and monitor the extractive industries in Africa.

CHAPTER 20

THE LAST WORD

The title of this chapter sounds ominous. Hopefully, it is not as final as it may sound. In fact, I would like to add to this title a caveat: it is the last word for this book only. Otherwise, "I will be back." At least, this is my hope as I reach the end of this book of stories from Africa. I would like to write more because I have enjoyed doing it.

I arrived in Africa when I was about twenty-one years old. That was 45 years ago. Writing these stories has allowed me to realize how much change I have witnessed in my lifetime and how much I have changed myself. From a young man who knew very little about life and even less about his own profession to becoming an experienced banker, crisscrossing the continents with courage and confidence... is how I wanted this book to unfold. It did not quite work out this way. I am happy that this book is not a saga of corporate conquests.

When I first arrived in Africa, I was expecting to be there for a period of three to four years and then move on to other parts of the world, just like regular expatriates. People still ask me what was the main cause of my lifelong attachment to Africa. It is not an easy question to answer for me, but I am going to attempt it here.

The initial shock of leaving my family home, my town, and my social and cultural surroundings lasted about a month. After that, I began to inquire and learn about my new surroundings. And there was so much to learn. As I tried to understand the history and geography of the country (Gabon) where I had landed, I was pulled into the intricacies of the politics and even the cultural scene of the continent. The mixing of ethnicities, languages, religions, and cultures that takes place in Africa was so different and so colorful for my young mind and my curious eyes that I was overwhelmed. This period of discovery began to change my life. The deep discomfort of leaving my home base began to dissipate as I connected with the new environment. It happened gradually. I quickly realized that the world is extremely complex and diverse. There was so much to learn and understand if I kept my mind focused on discovery and my eyes and ears open.

Often the sources of information were limited. There was no internet, no mobile phones and, of course, no artificial intelligence. There were no libraries in Gabon where I could go to read books of reference. Having conversations with knowledgeable people was my main source of learning. And I learned to listen to people. I was not accustomed to this. I had been a debater in my college life. I enjoyed heated debates with lively exchange of arguments and counterarguments. As a young bank officer, I was taught how to communicate with colleagues and clients. This training was focused on presenting a pitch and a corporate message. But my passion to learn about people and life in Africa required that I speak with people who had the relevant knowledge and experience. I quickly found out that such conversations required passive listening with occasional words of encouragement for the speaker. Once that format was well underway, I could ask a question, here and there, without any argumentation or debate. Whenever I had the opportunity, I would engage in such conversations with my colleagues, African friends, expats with some experience of living on the continent and, if I was lucky, meeting someone who had an academic background in social, cultural, or historical studies and research.

Within a short period of time, I found myself very much settled in Africa. I started to notice that when I traveled to Europe or my home country, very quickly, I would long to get back to my base in Africa. Being in Africa became my normal state of existence. Acquiring knowledge and understanding of my newfound environment was a key factor in achieving serenity in my life in Africa, but this was not the only reason. Another important reason was more down-to-earth. It was medical.

Paludism or malaria is endemic in tropical zones of Africa. The variety of malaria (caused by the parasite named "Plasmodium falciparum") in this part of the world is considered the most dangerous and harmful. I knew well about malaria because it existed in the Indian subcontinent. But it was a very mild sickness, similar to influenza. So, I was surprised when I was directed upon my arrival in Gabon to take antimalarial medicine on a regular basis. I learned that African malaria was something quite different and potentially deadly. I thus began to take the required weekly dose of chloroquine immediately. Within four weeks, however, the side effects of the pill became quite bothersome. I had nausea and stomach aches almost every day. People told me that I would get used to it. But two more weeks later, when things did not improve, I decided to see a doctor. I wanted to see an African doctor because I knew that the European doctors in Gabon would insist on chloroquine, no matter the side effects, due to their fear of serious consequences of malaria that included a possible cerebral version of the disease that could be fatal.

I managed to find an experienced Gabonese doctor who was actually a pediatrician, but he agreed to see me. He asked me where I grew up and how long I would be living in Gabon. I told him that I was from Pakistan, and I would be staying for several years in Gabon. He told me that the side effects would become worse and my life would be miserable. The only solution was to stop the weekly pill and avoid getting bitten by mosquitoes. I did not find this advice very helpful at first. But I gave it a try. Since 1979, I have not taken any antimalarial drug, and I have never caught malaria. So, not catching malaria is certainly a very important reason for my presence in Africa for so many years.

I have met many people who came to Africa for business or professional reasons and loved living here, but they ended up having to leave because they could not deal with persistent bouts of malaria.

After this very approximate analysis of the reasons why I settled in Africa, I can safely conclude that life in its essence is random. It just happens. In this short book, I have told some of the stories of my life in Africa. I have many more stories to tell, if the circumstances allow me to do so.

About the Author

Rizwan Haider is an international banker. His professional career spans more than 40 years. He lives in Benin, West Africa. He owns a consulting business and sits on the boards of directors of several banks, financial institutions, and an infrastructure company. He is also an adviser to the President of the Republic of Benin on banking and finance. In the past, he has held CEO positions in Ecobank and Orabank. He has also held senior positions in the HSBC group and Export Development Canada. He travels to Europe and North America frequently for family and business reasons.

Rizwan Haider grew up in Karachi, Pakistan. He moved to France and later to French-speaking Africa, working as an expatriate banker. He has lived and worked in several African countries, including France and Canada.

In his free time, he enjoys drawing, watercolor painting, and reading.